WHOLE BODY RESET DIET COOKBOOK

Your Weight-Loss Plan to Boost Your Metabolism, for a Flat Belly and Optimum Health at Midlife and Beyond, with Easy Recipes for 1000 Days and a 28-Day Smart Meal Plan

Written by:

Stephanie Miles & Maria F Rodriguez

Table of Contents

Chapter 1: Why Whole Body Reset Diet for a Flat Belly

We deal with weight gain and a rise in belly fat after the age of 40. Even with proper daily fitness and a balanced diet, we are unable to maintain our weight loss. What, on the other hand, should be the cause of this weight gain?

This is the right book for you to answer that question. It also details a tried-and-true, easy-to-follow method for reversing age-related weight and muscle loss, flattening your belly fat, and lowering your risk of disease, disability, and psychophysical deterioration.

Actually, there are so many diets that you can hardly count them anymore. You have probably already lost track and are wondering which diet is the best for achieving your goals and reduce that harmful belly fat. You have probably already tried one or that other method to get to grips with your hip gold. They should all be promising, from the cabbage soup diet to the pineapple diet. They aren't always due of their one-sidedness. Many individuals quit-up after only a few days since they can't see the specific meal they're meant to eat in large quantities. Who would want to eat pea soup every day?

The pound does drop swiftly on these "crash diets". However, you merely lose water at first. If your usual eating habits are resumed after diet, the yo-yo effect starts, and you acquire again weight. You went to such lengths. You rationed your diet and only ate the approved foods after that. You've gained even more weight! Isn't that inequitable?

The Whole Body Reset Diet is not an extreme diet and this is not even something you've ever tried before.

How many times you have been thinking: **"I Used to Have a Thin Body, but Now I have Not..."**

Take a moment now, wherever you are sitting, on the pillows of your sofa or in your bed, to consider your body and your current health. Take a peek at your stomach; is it bigger and fatter than it was before?

Belly fat makes people feel a variety of emotions. At "middle-age," you can take it as a personal attack.

Every day of our lives, this fat stands right there in front of you, refusing to go away. No matter how many physical workouts you do every day, how many "superfoods" you eat, or how many foods you avoid, belly fat will always be there—no amount of argument, begging, or bargaining can make it go away. In fact, we have a 200 percent increase in visceral fat from our 20s to our 60s, and visceral fat is the fat that lurks deep in our guts, hanging around our inner organs like rock-star groupies. Furthermore, whereas men's visceral belly fat increases by 200 percent, women's visceral belly fat increases by 400 percent.

Furthermore, whereas men's visceral belly fat increases by 200 percent, women's visceral belly fat increases by 400 percent.

If you've ever felt like this, I'm here to help you out with some helpful advice.

I was able to keep my weight in my life by following several diet trends and eating according to various dietary healthy programs. I've spent nearly my entire life attempting to get "the health and body that I desire and enjoy when I look in the mirror." I've also shed 20 pounds in two years after being overweight as a teenager.

Something unexpected happened in my life while I was in my forties. I was eating as I had always done, eating a complete, balanced, and healthy diet that had maintained me in the correct pant size up until that point, but my old clothes, my everyday pants and jeans, were no longer fitting properly. My stomach was expanding, despite the fact that I hadn't modified my food or exercise routine.

As a dietitian, I realized that belly fat was doing more than just making me look and feel horrible; we all know that belly fat is harmful for our health because visceral belly fat rests in our abdominal cavity, coating all of our inner organs, and it may be the cause of heart disease and stroke. Furthermore, belly fat produces inflammatory chemicals, which have been linked to diseases such as asthma, arteriosclerosis, autoimmune diseases, and Alzheimer's disease, as well as an increased risk of cancer (breast, colon, and prostate) and type 2 diabetes.

What my clients and I needed was a diet plan designed expressly for people whose belly fat had increased as a result of their age—an effective, sensible, and simple eating plan for people in their forties and fifties.

So, I researched and discovered this plan!

Many specialists who have researched the nutritional demands of people as they age say that current dietary guidelines and trends are so far off that they are possibly dangerous for people in their 40s and 50s and beyond. Surprisingly, there is a wealth of scientific data and information on how we should eat to reverse age-related weight gain, avoid age-related muscle loss, and, last but not least, maintain our long-term health.

Scientists name this dietary approach with the term of "Protein Timing."

The Protein Timing is a simple technique of eating that slows down age-related weight gain, maintains muscular tone, and slows down cellular "natural decline." The Whole Body Reset diet is a weight-loss program that has been scientifically demonstrated to be effective and safe for persons in their forties and fifties.

Chapter 2: The Whole Body Reset Weight-Loss Plan

The Whole Body Reset is based on the scientific premise that "Protein Timing"—eating the right quantity of protein at the right time of day—triggers the older body to avoid fat growth. This program also enhances muscle tissue health. This nutritional strategy, when combined with a variety of high-quality proteins, vitamins, fiber, and minerals, as well as healthy fats, can help people improve not just their bodies but also their lives.

Yet, once you understand how to eat according to the theory of Protein Timing and incorporate it into your daily life, you can lose up to 25 pounds in just 12 weeks—the majority of which comes from pure fat and belly fat—while also boosting metabolism, preserving muscle mass and tone, and positively impacting blood pressure and our well-being markers (blood sugar, blood cholesterol, and blood pressure).

This program can also help to lower the risk of many chronic illnesses associated with aging, as well as improve overall brain and body health.

The Whole Body Reset program is easy to follow:

- **You can eat what you want.** There is no strange scientific evidence that says we can't eat specific foods like beans, milk, bread, tomatoes, chocolate, sweets, or whatever else we choose. This isn't a ketogenic, low-carb, low-sugar, or low-fat diet. There are no foods that are "off-limits." There are no calorie counters or metrics to keep track of. You're not obligated to eat things that don't match your lifestyle or suit your body—whether you're a vegan, vegetarian, diabetic, or simply don't like fish or eggplant, the Whole Body Reset nutritional program will allow you to eat properly.

- **You can eat normal foods.** There are no specialty meals, unusual items, or "superfoods" to buy—just wonderful food from your neighborhood store and favorite restaurant (including fast food!).

- **You can eat when you want.** You don't have to fast, cleanse, or fast intermittently during the day, limiting yourself to "on" or "off" hours.

- **This program is healthy.** It's also safe and effective, with renowned scientists in the fields of weight loss, weight management, aging, and nutrition approving it.

Chapter 3: Top 10 Benefits of the Whole Body Reset Program

1. Prevent, slow, and reverse weight gain as you get older.

2. Support and regulate our immune system.

3. Prevent and reverse muscle loss as you get older.

4. Assist in the prevention of atherosclerosis and loss of mobility.

5. Maintain the health of your bones and joints.

6. Enhance cognitive abilities.

7. Maintain cardiovascular health by keeping blood pressure low.

8. Increase the absorption of vital macro and micronutrients through improving intestinal health.

9. Maintain a low blood sugar level and blood sugar stability.

10. Increase vigor, engagement, and vigilance.

The Whole Body Reset diet represents a simple way of eating that will help you to reverse age-related muscle loss—even during weight loss or when you're burning fat. The hypothesis of "Protein Timing" is not a new concept and it is not a gimmick. Protein Timing is a long-term proven approach that aims to maintain and gradually increase lean muscle tissue. Mostly, this method has been used by young athletes to improve their performance, including muscular power, strength, endurance, and cardiovascular health.

However, scientific data reveals that as we age, particularly in our 40s and 50s, timing our protein intake is no longer merely a question of being able to run faster or leap higher. Protein Timing becomes essential to maintaining us healthy, slim, trim, and disease-free when we consider how our bodies evolve over time. Eating the proper quantity of protein at specified intervals results in considerable weight loss with no rebound effect. Adults in their 50s got stronger and slimmer after starting the Protein Timing program, according to one research.

Simply increasing our protein intake to 25–30 g each meal will cause our bodies to behave in the same manner as a younger body would. According to recent research, when persons in their 60s mixed a high-quality protein meal with resistance training, their bodies responded in the same manner as those in their 20s did.

Researchers recommend that older individuals consume 1–1.2 g of protein per kg of body weight—roughly 0.5–0.6 g per pound. However, they also showed that 25–30 g of protein each meal was a critical threshold for elderly adults to attain anabolic maintenance—the point at which muscle may be preserved.

The Whole Body Reset plan, however, does not include a "high-protein diet." The average daily protein dosage with this program is not significantly more than with a typical diet, but what will happen is that "the concentration and timing of protein intake" will shift throughout the day. The end product will be spectacular!

Protein Timing begins at breakfast for those in their forties and fifties. Researchers discovered that women who consume less than 25 g of protein for breakfast (less than 30 g for males) will remain in "muscle-loss" mode for the rest of the day. So, whether you start your day with nothing more than a croissant and coffee, or fruit and a bowl of oatmeal or cereals, you'll be taking that single critical step on your midlife weight-loss path to enhance your first meal of the day. To start your day off right, make sure you eat lots of protein-rich breakfast foods—easy and quick options you can make at home or get at your favorite restaurant or bar.

Are you too preoccupied to cook? You may build muscle by drinking one of our protein-rich smoothies. Breakfast smoothies are the quickest, simplest, and most delicious way to reset your entire body for weight loss and muscle gain. Even if you aren't a big fan of dairy. Let me reiterate: a conventional healthy breakfast, even if you're eating the high-fiber oat-bran cereals recommended by your doctor, is insufficiently healthy. Not for individuals in their forties and fifties.

Chapter 4: The Principles of the Whole Body Reset Program

Number of Meals

3 (breakfast, lunch, and dinner)

Number of Snacks

1–2.

It is recommended to eat at each meal (including breakfast) at least 25 g of proteins for women and 30 g for men. Snacks have to give you an additional 7 g or more of proteins and 2 g or more of fiber.

Foods to Include

Vegetables

It's advisable to eat 4-5 servings of vegetables per day. Vegetables are rich source of magnesium, vitamins, potassium, and fiber. Also pay attention to the nutritional content of each food. Beans are a good choice as they have a proper nutritional value. Sweet potatoes are high in Vitamin A, plus fiber that boost the functionality of blood vessels. Other options include winter squash, cauliflower, broccoli, spinach, carrots, kale, beetroot, garlic, onion, and tomatoes.

Fruits

Just like vegetables, you need to eat at least 4-5 servings of fruit for fiber and essential energy that promotes the proper functioning of the bod. You can have your fruits dried, frozen, canned, or fresh. For canned fruits, make sure you have read the nutritional label to check whether there's any added sugar. Most fruits are good sources of magnesium, fiber, potassium, and low-fat content. You can also include common fruits as part of this diet, including apples, raisins, pineapples, oranges, and melons.

Whole Grains

You should have 7-8 servings of whole grains of whole grains daily to boost your nutrient and fiber intake.

You can consider various cereals. Pasta and bread but avoid topping them with cheese, cream, or butter. Also consider include whole-wheat pasta, brown rice, popcorn, whole oats, quinoa, and whole-wheat bread.

Dairy Products

When choosing the dairy products for your diet consider both low-fat and fat-free dairy products. Dairy is an excellent source of Vitamin D, calcium, and protein. They can be a cup of yogurt, milk, or 1.5 ounces of cheese. Other options include low-fat milk, skim, or fat-free milk, low-fat cheese or fat-free cheese, and low-fat yogurt, and fat-free yogurt. Milk contains nutrients that are critical for the absorption of potassium, calcium and Vitamin D.

Lean and High-Quality Proteins

You need to have at least 3 servings of poultry, lean meat, or fish daily. Lean and skinless meat are excellent sources of vitamin B complex, zinc, iron, and protein. Some of the choices you can consider include seafood and fish that give you Omega 3 and help in lowering your cholesterol levels. However, you should aim for fresh food as opposed to canned to limit salt intake and preservatives. You can bake, grill, or roast but try to limit frying. Other options are eggs with one egg making up one serving and lean poultry (always ensure you remove the skin).

Nuts

When making a weekly meal plan be sure to include 5-6 servings of beans, legumes, nuts, and seeds. These are a good source of magnesium, phytochemicals, protein, and fiber. Since most of these contain high calories, make sure you watch your count. A single serving can be 2 tablespoons of nuts. Some of the common foods of this group are pistachios, lentils, kidney beans, peas, cashews, peanuts, and almonds, among others.

Fats and oils

According to nutritionists, you need to include 2-3 fats and oils servings every day. These are essentials in strengthening the immune system and absorbing nutrients. Even then, you must exercise caution and control the amount you will use because when left uncontrolled, excessive fats and oils can result in being obese,

The onset of diabetes, and cardiovascular diseases. One serving can be a teaspoon of mayonnaise or a tablespoon of salad dressing, soft margarine, or vegetable oil. Other options include coconut oil, extra-virgin olive oil, and peanut.

Sugars and Sweets

Surprise! The Whole Body Reset Diet allows you to have a maximum of 5 servings or less of sugar per week. This plan doesn't restrict you from sweet completely. However, you must aim for those that are low in fat content. Some perfect examples that make up a serving would be jelly beans, low-fat granola cookies, or bars, or fruit ice. Several sweeteners you can consider include sugar, raw honey, agave syrup, and maple syrup. Most of these are mostly natural sweeteners hence a good choice.

Secret Good Habits

Protein breakfast smoothies. They can help you make every day a muscle-building and fat-burning day.

Foods to Avoid

Highly processed foods and caloric drinks. Yet, do not worry, you will not be deprived! In this diet, you'll find lots of ready-to-eat treats that you can buy in online stores or at your local supermarket.

Exercise

Walking, running, swimming, cycling, hiking, dancing in the house—anything that fits your body, lifestyle, and preferred form of exercise—along with some resistance and strength training. Thirty minutes of training per day, five days per week is recommended.

Chapter 5: The Benefits of the Whole Body Reset Diet

The Whole Body Reset diet represents a simple way of eating that will help you to reverse age-related muscle loss—even during weight loss or when you're burning fat. The hypothesis of "Protein Timing" is not a new concept and it is not a gimmick. Protein Timing is a long-term proven approach that aims to maintain and gradually increase lean muscle tissue. Mostly, this method has been used by young athletes to improve their performance, including muscular power, strength, endurance, and cardiovascular health.

Prevention of Cardiovascular Diseases and Hypertension

People with blood pressure readings exceeding 140/90 mmHg are more likely to have a heart attack as well as develop vascular diseases. Blood pressure can be reduced without medication by following a good diet and losing weight. Of course, this is a far healthier way for you to manage your high blood pressure as. Drugs, after all, usually have side effects.

Moreover, belly fat is dangerous as it can reach the coronaries causing stroke by coronary occlusion. Therefore, by reducing your belly fat, you'll reduce also the risk of cardiovascular diseases.

Assist in the Prevention of Metabolic Syndrome

Blood pressure, blood sugar, triglycerides, bad cholesterol, and insulin resistance are all reduced by weight loss and belly fat decrease. For people suffering from metabolic syndrome, obesity, or type 2 diabetes, this is a dream come true. For people with metabolic syndrome, you'll notice changes in your blood pressure points and systolic pressure in just few weeks.

Getting in Shape

Starting the Whole Body reset Diet doesn't have to be only about losing weight, as the most important effect is the reduction of visceral fat. This diet avoids things that can cause weight gain and is reaching proteins to build a proper muscle tone. Moreover, despite being taught that three meals a day is the golden rule, eating a variety of meals throughout the day allows your metabolism to work smarter, not harder, to help you lose weight.

Immune System Strengthening

Food's high in antioxidants is included in the Whole Body Reset diet. These dietary groups assist your body in producing antioxidants to protect your cells from free radicals. Antioxidants can help you avoid cancer, heart disease, and other serious diseases by boosting your immune system and keeping you safe.

Chapter 6: What to Expect from the Whole Body Reset Diet

This isn't one of those classic diets where you "go on" one day and "go off" the next. You won't have a yo-yo effect, where you lose weight and then gain it again. The Whole Body Reset diet is a long-term, sustainable way of eating that can help you reverse age-related weight gain and muscle loss. This is not a deprivation diet; instead, it focuses on increasing the number of healthful, life-sustaining meals you consume on a regular basis. At a birthday party, you can eat sweets and cake, and you don't have to hide under the table when the pizza arrives. To maintain your body strong and lean, all you have to do is make sure you eat the right nutrients every day.

Benefits of the Food You'll Eat in this Dietary Approach

- **Proteins**: Eggs, fish, seafood, crustaceans, low-fat meat, poultry, a combination of whole grains and legumes, milk and plant-based milk, yogurt and kefir, cottage and seasoned cheese, and a mixture of whole grains and legumes Proteins are the fundamental components of our bodies, including organs, muscle, skin appendages, and even DNA. Protein deficiency causes a slowed metabolism, which leads to weight gain, weakened immunity, inadequate muscular growth, depression, and other issues. If you're overweight, it's almost probably due to a diet that's low in protein and rich in carbs and sugar.

- **Fibers**: Fruits, legumes, and vegetables, as well as wholegrain pasta and bread. Carbohydrates comprise fibers, which provide energy to our bodies. Nonetheless, knowing how to dose carbs is critical, as an overabundance of them will raise blood sugar levels and body fat. Fibers are a significant source of health when consumed in the correct diets because they support good gut function and lower blood cholesterol.

- **Healthy fats**: Extra-virgin olive oil, peanut oil, sesame oil, coconut oil, dried fruits, seeds, natural peanut butter (no additional oil or sugar), avocado, and olives are some of the ingredients. EPA, DHA, and omega-3 essential fatty acids are the most well-known fatty acids, which are mostly found in fish. These aid in the reduction of cholesterol, the reduction of inflammation, the enhancement of cognitive capacities, the reduction of free radicals, and the enhancement of vision. In addition, extra-virgin olive oil is essential for heart and circulatory health. It is a valuable ally for reducing inflammation in our bodies because it is high in vitamin E.

- **Vitamins and minerals**: Calcium, potassium, and magnesium, as well as vitamins A, B12, C, D, and E. They all have anti-oxidant properties, stimulate skin regeneration by boosting collagen formation, reduce stress, and strengthen our immune system.

So, get ready for this weight-loss, muscle-building revolution! The Whole Body Reset diet is here to help you!

Chapter 7: Your Basic Shopping List

Dairy Products

Aim for two to three dairy products daily to acquire critical nutrients, including protein, calcium, fats, and Vitamin D. These are some of those choices with the suggested types and amounts that shouldbe:

- Cheese - 1.5 oz. serving
- Fat-free - 1% milk - skim - 1 cup
- Yogurt or frozen yogurt - 1 cup

Milk provides an assortment of high-quality proteins to increase calcium concentration. If lactose is your enemy, choose almond and coconut milk since neither one contains dairy properties.

Some research studies have found people can combat unwanted weight gain with a serving of yogurt added to your diet plan each day. You'll also attain excellent intestinal bacteria to achieve and sustain an improved weight regimen.

Vegetables

It is important to eat four to five vegetable servings daily for fiber, vitamins, potassium, and magnesium. Always check the nutrients and avoid sodium. Here are several suggestions:

- Winter Squash are an excellent alternative for pasta dishes to lower the calorie content, servedas spaghetti squash.
- Sweet Potatoes contain vitamin A and fiber to boost your blood vessel health.
- Beans are a great option but put white beans at the top of your shopping list. Always thoroughly rinse canned beans to lower their sodium content.
- Broccoli: These delicious 'mini trees' provide you with tons of benefits, including decreasing your risk of overall mortality, diabetes, heart disease, and obesity. It's an excellent way to promote a healthy complexion and boost beautiful hair. You will also have increased energy and overall weight loss.

Other Vegetable Choices

- Arugula - About 2 cups - 40 grams - 10 calories

- Cauliflower - boiled - 100 grams - 28 calories

- Kale - 100 grams of raw kale - 28 calories or boiled - 24 calories

- Carrots - 1 medium - 25 calories

- Boiled lima beans - 1 tbsp. - 13 calories

- Green beans - 100 grams - 23.5 calories

- Spinach - 100 grams - 23.2 calories

- Beets - 1 cup - 59 calories

- Garlic - 100 grams - 149 calories

- Scallion - 1 to 5 grams – 5 calories

- Shallot – 1 to 43 grams- 31 calories

- Fresh Tomatoes – 100 grams – 17.7 calories

Fruits

Nutritionists advise four or five helpings of fruit each day to ensure crucial fiber intake and boost your energy levels. Choose from fresh, frozen, or dried, while making sure to check each of the ingredient/nutrition panels for salt or sugar content.

Most fruits include substantial amounts of magnesium, potassium, and numerous are minimal in fat. Consider these serving portions as an example:

- Frozen- fresh fruit – ½ cup portion

- Fruit Juice – enjoy ½ cup

- Fruit – 1 medium of choice
- Dried Fruit – ¼ cup serving

Enjoy these (listed with approximate calorie content for your convenience):

- Bananas will provide roughly 13 percent of your daily potassium needs. Therefore, have a serving if you have issues with leg cramps. After all, one medium banana is merely 105 calories.
- Apples are high in fiber and antioxidants. Two extra small apples are 105 calories.
- Pears are high in fiber content and an excellent antioxidant (102 calories for one medium or 178 grams).

These are a few more to consider:

- Apricots - 6 whole - 101 calories
- Peaches – 2 and ½ medium – 96 calories
- Fates – 1 and ½ each – 100 calories
- Grapes – 30 – 101 calories
- Sliced mangoes – 1 cup – 101 calories
- Oranges – 2 small – 90 calories
- Cantaloupe Melons – 2 cups diced – 106 calories
- Nectarines 1 and ½ - 94 calories
- Pineapples – 1 and ½ cups cut in chunks – 103 calories
- Raisins – 1 small box about 1 and 1/ oz – 129 calories
- Strawberries – 25 medium – 96 calories
- Tangerines – 2 medium – 100 calories
- Raspberries – 1 and ½ cups or about 100 berries   96 calories
- Blueberries – ½ cups pr about 125 berries – 103 calories
- Blackberries – 100 berries or 1 and ½ cups – 100 calories

Nuts – Seeds and Legumes

While you're making your plan for the week, be sure to include 5 to 6 servings of seeds, nuts, beans, and legumes. Healthy veggies will provide you with additional protein, magnesium, phytochemicals, and fiber. Some may have higher calorie counts. One serving could be .5 cup of cooked legumes, 1.5 ounces or .33 cup of nuts, two tablespoons of nut butter, or .5 ounces or two tablespoons of seeds. Consider some of these options:

- Almonds - 622 calories per 100 grams
- Kidney beans - 215 calories per one cup - 256 grams
- Peas - 125 calories per one cup - 160 grams
- Pistachios - 170 calories per ½ cup
- Cashews - 585 calories per 100 grams
- Peanuts - 427 calories per 73 grams or for each .5 cup

Whole Grains

You should consume 100% whole grains daily (7-8 portions). Select a variety of pasta, cereals, or bread. Steer clear of butter, cheese, or cream. Try one of the following:

- Quinoa – always rinse them prior to cooking – 1 cup cooked – 222 calories
- Brown rice – per cooked cup – 218 calories
- Whole oats – ex. Steel cut oats – per ¼ cup dry – 150 calories
- Popcorn – ¼ cup – makes 10 cup – 248 calories

Protein Choices

It's advisable to enjoy up to six servings of poultry, fish, or lean meat each day. One ounce of cooked fish, seafood, and meat - roasted, baked, or grilled - is an ap- propriate amount, but you should avoid frying the options. Skinless - lean meat is a good source for zinc, B complex vitamins, protein, and iron. Consider choosing these:

Seafood & Fish: Omega 3 fatty acids are present in tuna, salmon, and herring, to assist in lowering your blood cholesterol levels. Select fresh clams to minimize salt and the intake of unnecessary preservatives. Poultry is another lean option but always remember to remove the skin. Eggs: 1 egg is one serving. Dietitians recommend consuming a bare minimum of two to three servings of fats or oils in your diet plan each day. Consider a serving as one teaspoon of vegetable oil, mayo, or soft margarine. You can also choose from coconut, peanut, or extra- virgin olive oil (EVOO).

Sweetener Options

The Whole Body reset Diet allows five portions/servings (maximum) each week. Weekly, you're permitted a maximum of five servings or less of sugar.

- Raw Honey: Honey can be purchased raw honey as a comb, and in products that are spreadable and whipped.
- Maple Syrup: The natural sugar is high in calcium content.
- Sugar: According to the American Heart Association, women are allowed 25 grams daily, whereby men are allowed 36 grams of sugar, which is about the same scale as considered by WHO. However, the average American will consume 82 grams of added sugar every single day. Consider this as a scale. One tablespoon of jam or jelly or 1/2 cup of sorbet will equal one tablespoon of sugar.
- Agave Syrup: This syrup is also sometimes called agave nectar and is a native of Mexico. It resembles honey - but it is even sweeter, fruitier, and has a much cleaner flavor. It can be in anything from BBQ sauce to catch it to baked goods or ice cream.

Chapter 9:
Drinks and Smoothies for Whole Body Reset Diet

Chapter 9: Drink and Smoothie Recipes

9.1 Super Green Juice

TIME TO PREPARE
5 minutes

COOK TIME
0 minutes

SERVING
2 people

Nutritional Facts
57 kcal
8 gr Prot.

Ingredients

- 1 green apple
- ¼ cup broccoli
- ¼ cup mint
- 1 cucumber
- ¼ cup coriander
- 1 lettuce leave
- ¼ celery leaves
- ½ cup ice cubes
- 1 water
- 1 tsp Stevia sweetener

Steps to Cook

1. First, take all the green vegetables and the green apple and wash them properly with water.
2. Now take the blender and put the above ingredients in it.
3. Then add ice cubes, water, and stevia sweetener. Switch on the blender and mix all ingredients very well.
4. Now pour super green juice into glasses and serve it.

Chapter 9: Drink and Smoothie Recipes

9.2 Carrot Juice

TIME TO PREPARE

5 minutes

COOK TIME

0 minutes

SERVING

2 people

Nutritional facts

37 kcal

8 gr Prot.

Ingredients

- 4 carrots
- 1 orange
- 1 tsp black pepper
- 1 tbsp lemon juice

Steps to Cook

1. First, take carrots and wash them properly. Then peel the vegetables.
2. Take a juicer and add carrots to it and make juice of it.
3. Now add orange juice, black pepper, and lemon juice and mix them very well.
4. Now pour carrot juice into glasses and serve it.

Chapter 9: Drink and Smoothie Recipes

9.3 Watermelon Juice

TIME TO PREPARE

5 minutes

COOK TIME

0 minutes

SERVING

2 people

Nutritional Facts

19 kcal

10 gr Prot.

Ingredients

- 2 cups watermelon
- ¼ cup mint leaves
- ¼ cup lemon juice
- 1 cup ice cubes

Steps to Cook

1. Rinse watermelon with water and then cut it into pieces and then remove seeds from it.
2. Now take a blender and add watermelon cubes and ice cubes and blend it till it mixes very well.
3. Now add mint leaves and lemon juice and blend it again.
4. Now pour watermelon juice into glasses and serve it.

Chapter 9: Drink and Smoothie Recipes

9.4 Flat Belly Cantaloupe Juice

TIME TO PREPARE

5 minutes

COOK TIME

0 minutes

SERVING

2 people

Nutritional Facts

28 kcal

8 gr Prot.

Ingredients

- 2 cups cantaloupe
- ¼ cup mint leaves
- ¼ cup lemon juice
- 1 cup ice cubes
- 1 tsp black pepper

Steps to Cook

1. Rinse cantaloupe with water and cut it into pieces. Then remove seeds from it.
2. Now take a blender and add cantaloupe cubes and ice cubes and blend it till it mixes very well.
3. Now add mint leaves, black pepper, and lemon juice and blend it again.
4. Now pour cantaloupe juice into glasses and serve it.

Chapter 9: Drink and Smoothie Recipes

9.5 Flat Belly Pomegranate Juice

TIME TO PREPARE
5 minutes

COOK TIME
0 minutes

SERVING
2 people

Nutritional Facts
100 kcal
8 gr Prot.

Ingredients

- 2 cups pomegranate
- Salt to taste
- ¼ cup water

Steps to Cook

1. Take a blender and add pomegranate and put some water in it and blend it properly.
2. Now pass this juice from the sieve and remove seeds from it.
3. Add a pinch of salt to it and serve it in the glasses for a weight-loss drink.

Chapter 9: Drink and Smoothie Recipes

9.6 Amla Juice

TIME TO PREPARE

5 minutes

COOK TIME

0 minutes

SERVING

2 people

Nutritional Facts

102 kcal

8 gr Prot.

Ingredients

- 3–4 amla
- 2 cups water
- Salt to taste
- 1 tsp black pepper
- 1 tsp ginger

Steps to Cook

1. Take amla and cut it into small cubes.
2. Add this to the blender and add water, salt, ginger, and black pepper. Blend it very well.
3. Take out the amla juice in glasses and serve it as a weight-loss drink.

Chapter 9: Drink and Smoothie Recipes

9.7 Chia Seeds Lemonade

TIME TO PREPARE

5 minutes

COOK TIME

0 minutes

SERVING

2 people

Nutritional Facts

27 kcal

6 gr Prot.

Ingredients

- 2 glasses of lukewarm water
- 2 tbsp lemon juice
- 2 tbsp chia seeds
- 1 tbsp celery leaves

Steps to Cook

1. Take lukewarm water in a jug.
2. Add lemon juice to it and mix it very well.
3. Then add chia seeds to it and mix it again.
4. Add celery leaves and give it a final mix.
5. Take out chia seeds lemonade in glasses and garnish it with lemon slices and serve it as a weight-loss drink.

9.8 Beetroot Juice

TIME TO PREPARE

5 minutes

COOK TIME

0 minutes

SERVING

2 people

Nutritional Facts

54 kcal

8 gr Prot.

Ingredients

- 2 cups beetroot
- Salt to taste
- Black pepper to taste
- 2 cups water

Steps to Cook

1. Take a blender and add beetroot and put some water in it and blend it properly.
2. Add a pinch of salt to it.
3. Then add black pepper to it and serve it in the glasses as a weight-loss drink.

Chapter 9: Drink and Smoothie Recipes

9.9 Detox Green Juice

TIME TO PREPARE

5 minutes

COOK TIME

0 minutes

SERVING

2 people

Nutritional Facts

97 kcal

8 gr Prot.

Ingredients

- 1 green apple
- 1 grapefruit
- ¼ cup mint
- 1 cucumber
- ¼ cup spinach leaves
- ¼ cup lemon juice
- ½ cup ice cubes
- 1 water
- 1 tsp honey

Steps to Cook

1. First, take all ingredients and wash them properly with water.
2. Now take the water and add the apple, the grapefruit, the mint, the cucumber, and the spinach and soak them overnight.
3. Now take the blender and add the detox water to it. Then add ice cubes, water, honey, and lemon juice. Switch on the blender and mix all ingredients very well.
4. Now take out detox green juice in glasses and serve it.

Chapter 9: Drink and Smoothie Recipes

9.10 Orange Detox Juice

TIME TO PREPARE

5 minutes

COOK TIME

0 minutes

SERVING

2 people

Nutritional Facts

97 kcal

10 gr Prot.

Ingredients

- 2 carrots
- 1 cup orange juice
- ¼ cup mint leaves
- ¼ cup lemon juice
- 1 cup ice cubes
- 1 tsp black pepper

Steps to Cook

1. Rinse carrots with water and then cut them into pieces.
2. Now take a blender and add carrot cubes, orange juice, and ice cubes and blend it till it mixes very well.
3. Now add mint leaves, black pepper, and lemon juice and blend it again.
4. Now pour orange detox juice into glasses and serve it.

Chapter 9: Drink and Smoothie Recipes

9.11 Tropical Carrot Apple Juice

TIME TO PREPARE

5 minutes

COOK TIME

0 minutes

SERVING

2 people

Nutritional Facts

95 kcal

8 gr Prot.

Ingredients

- 2 carrots
- 2 apples
- 1 cup orange juice
- 1 ginger cube
- ¼ cup lemon juice
- 1 cup ice cubes
- 1 tsp black pepper

Steps to Cook

1. Rinse carrots and apples with water and then cut them into pieces.

2. Now take a blender and add carrot cubes, apple cubes, orange juice, 1 ginger cube, and ice cubes and blend them till they mix very well.

3. Now add black pepper and lemon juice and blend it again.

4. Now pour tropical carrot-apple juice into glasses and serve it.

Chapter 9: Drink and Smoothie Recipes

9.12 Zesty Lemon Apple Drink

TIME TO PREPARE

5 minutes

COOK TIME

0 minutes

SERVING

2 people

Nutritional Facts

47 kcal

6 gr Prot.

Ingredients

- 2 apples
- 1 tsp lemon zest
- ¼ cup lemon juice
- 1 cup ice cubes
- 1 tsp black pepper

Steps to Cook

1. Rinse apples with water and then cut them into pieces and remove seeds from them.
2. Now take a blender and add apple cubes, lemon zest, and ice cubes and blend them till they mix properly.
3. Now add black pepper and lemon juice and blend it again.
4. Now pour zesty lemon apple juice into glasses and serve it.

Chapter 9: Drink and Smoothie Recipes

9.13 Green Spinach Lemonade

TIME TO PREPARE

5 minutes

COOK TIME

0 minutes

SERVING

2 people

Nutritional Facts

27 kcal

8 gr Prot.

Ingredients

- 1 cup spinach
- ¼ cup mint leaves
- ¼ cup lemon juice
- 1 cup ice cubes
- 1 tsp black pepper

Steps to Cook

1. Rinse spinach with water and then cut it into pieces.
2. Now take a blender and add spinach and ice cubes and blend it till it mixes properly.
3. Now add mint leaves, black pepper, and lemon juice and blend it again.
4. Now pour green spinach lemonade into glasses and serve it.

Chapter 9: Drink and Smoothie Recipes

9.14 Green Apple Juice

TIME TO PREPARE

5 minutes

COOK TIME

0 minutes

SERVING

2 people

Nutritional Facts

46 kcal

6 gr Prot.

Ingredients

- 2 green apples
- ¼ cup lemon juice
- 1 cup ice cubes
- 1 tsp black pepper

Steps to Cook

1. Rinse green apples with water and then cut them into pieces and remove seeds from them.
2. Now take a blender and add apple cubes and ice cubes and blend it till it mixes properly.
3. Now add black pepper and lemon juice and blend it again.
4. Now pour green apple juice into glasses and serve it.

Chapter 9: Drink and Smoothie Recipes

9.15 Grapefruit Juice

TIME TO PREPARE

5 minutes

COOK TIME

0 minutes

SERVING

2 people

Nutritional Facts

75 kcal

8 gr Prot.

Ingredients

- 4 grapefruits
- ¼ cup mint leaves
- ¼ cup lemon juice
- 1 cup ice cubes
- 1 tsp black pepper

Steps to Cook

1. Peel grapefruits.
2. Now take a blender and add grapefruit cubes and ice cubes and blend it till it mixes properly
3. Now add mint leaves, black pepper, and lemon juice and blend it again.
4. Now pour grapefruit juice into glasses and serve it.

Chapter 9: Drink and Smoothie Recipes

9.16 Red Grapes Juice

TIME TO PREPARE

5 minutes

COOK TIME

0 minutes

SERVING

2 people

Nutritional Facts

55 kcal

8 gr Prot.

Ingredients

- 2 cups red grapes
- ¼ cup mint leaves
- ¼ cup lemon juice
- 1 cup ice cubes
- 1 tsp black pepper

Steps to Cook

1. Rinse red grapes with water.

2. Now take a blender and add red grapes and ice cubes and blend it till it mixes properly.

3. Now add mint leaves, black pepper, and lemon juice and blend it again.

4. Now pour red grape juice into glasses and serve it.

Chapter 9: Drink and Smoothie Recipes

9.17 Strawberry Cooler

TIME TO PREPARE

5 minutes

COOK TIME

0 minutes

SERVING

2 people

Nutritional Facts

45 kcal

8 gr Prot.

Ingredients

- 2 cups strawberries
- ½ cup pomegranate
- ¼ cup mint leaves
- ¼ cup lemon juice
- 1 cup ice cubes
- 1 tsp black pepper

Steps to Cook

1. Rinse strawberries with water and then cut them into pieces.
2. Now take a blender and add strawberry cubes, pomegranate, and ice cubes and blend it till it mixes properly.
3. Now add mint leaves, black pepper, and lemon juice and blend it again.
4. Now pour the strawberry cooler into glasses and serve it.

Chapter 9: Drink and Smoothie Recipes

9.18 Blueberry Juice

TIME TO PREPARE

5 minutes

COOK TIME

0 minutes

SERVING

2 people

Nutritional Facts

65 kcal

8 gr Prot.

Ingredients	Steps to Cook

Ingredients

- 2 cups blueberry
- ¼ cup mint leaves
- ¼ cup lemon juice
- 1 cup ice cubes
- 1 tsp black pepper

Steps to Cook

1. Rinse blueberry with water.

2. Now take a blender and add blueberry and ice cubes and blend it till it mixes properly.

3. Now add mint leaves, black pepper, and lemon juice and blend it again.

4. Now pour blueberry juice into glasses and serve it.

Chapter 9: Drink and Smoothie Recipes

9.19 Kiwi Splash

TIME TO PREPARE

5 minutes

COOK TIME

0 minutes

SERVING

2 people

Nutritional Facts

67 kcal

6 gr Prot.

Ingredients

- 2 cups kiwi
- ¼ cup mint leaves
- ¼ cup lemon juice
- 1 cup ice cubes
- 1 tsp black pepper

Steps to Cook

1. Rinse the kiwi with water and then cut it into pieces.

2. Now take a blender and add kiwi cubes and ice cubes and blend it till it mixes properly.

3. Now add mint leaves, black pepper, and lemon juice and blend it again.

4. Now pour the kiwi splash into glasses and serve it.

Chapter 9: Drink and Smoothie Recipes

9.20 Flat Belly Pineapple Juice

TIME TO PREPARE

5 minutes

COOK TIME

0 minutes

SERVING

2 people

Nutritional Facts

57 kcal

6 gr Prot.

Ingredients

- 2 cups pineapple
- ¼ cup mint leaves
- ¼ cup lemon juice
- 1 cup ice cubes
- 1 tsp black pepper

Steps to Cook

1. Rinse pineapple with water and then cut it into pieces.

2. Now take a blender and add pineapple cubes and ice cubes and blend it till it mixes properly.

3. Now add mint leaves, black pepper, and lemon juice and blend it again.

4. Now pour flat belly pineapple juice into glasses and serve it.

Chapter 9: Drink and Smoothie Recipes

9.21 Raspberry Weight-Loss Smoothie

TIME TO PREPARE

5 minutes

COOK TIME

0 minutes

SERVING

2 people

Nutritional Facts

117 kcal

8 gr Prot.

Ingredients

- 1 cup raspberry
- Mint leaves for garnish
- 1 cup fat-free yogurt
- ½ cup ice cubes
- ½ cup skim milk

Steps to Cook

1. Add raspberries, fat-free yogurt, ice cubes, and skim milk into the blender.
2. Blend the compound until smooth.
3. Pour into the glasses and top with mint and garnish it with raspberry and serve it.

Chapter 9: Drink and Smoothie Recipes

9.22 Coconut Cashew Protein Smoothie

TIME TO PREPARE

5 minutes

COOK TIME

0 minutes

SERVING

2 people

Nutritional Facts

134 kcal

8 gr Prot.

Ingredients

- ¼ shredded coconut
- Mint leaves for garnish
- 1 cup fat-free yogurt
- ½ cup ice cubes
- ½ cup coconut milk

Steps to Cook

1. Add coconut, fat-free yogurt, ice cubes, and coconut milk into the blender.
2. Blend until smooth.
3. Pour into the glasses and top with mint and garnish it with coconut slices and serve it.

Chapter 9: Drink and Smoothie Recipes

9.23 Kale Recharge Smoothie

TIME TO PREPARE

5 minutes

COOK TIME

0 minutes

SERVING

2 people

Nutritional Facts

137 kcal

8 gr Prot.

Ingredients

- 1 cup kale
- Mint leaves for garnish
- 1 cup low-fat yogurt
- ½ cup ice cubes
- ½ cup skim milk

Steps to Cook

1. Add kale, low-fat yogurt, ice cubes, and skim milk into the blender.
2. Blend the compound until smooth.
3. Pour into the glasses and top with mint and garnish it with kale and serve it.
4. Enjoy!

9.24 Peach Cobbler

TIME TO PREPARE

5 minutes

COOK TIME

0 minutes

SERVING

2 people

Nutritional Facts

146 kcal

6 gr Prot.

Ingredients

- 1 cup peach cubes
- Mint leaves for garnish
- 1 cup low-fat yogurt
- ½ cup ice cubes
- ½ cup skim milk

Steps to Cook

1. Add peaches, low-fat yogurt, ice cubes, and skim milk into the blender.
2. Blend until smooth.
3. Pour into the glasses and top with mint and garnish it with peach slices and serve it.
4. Enjoy!

Chapter 9: Drink and Smoothie Recipes

9.25 Banana Split

TIME TO PREPARE

5 minutes

COOK TIME

0 minutes

SERVING

2 people

Nutritional Facts

134 kcal

8 gr Prot.

Ingredients	Steps to Cook
• 1 cup banana cubes • Mint leaves for garnish • 1 cup low-fat yogurt • ½ cup ice cubes • ½ cup skim milk	1. Add banana cubes, low-fat yogurt, ice cubes, and skim milk into the blender. 2. Blend until smooth. 3. Pour into the glasses and top with mint and garnish it with banana slices and serve it. 4. Enjoy!

Chapter 9: Drink and Smoothie Recipes

9.26 Almond Shake

TIME TO PREPARE

5 minutes

COOK TIME

0 minutes

SERVING

2 people

Nutritional Facts

145 kcal

8 gr Prot.

Ingredients

- ½ cup almonds
- Mint leaves for garnish
- 1 cup low-fat yogurt
- ½ cup ice cubes
- ½ cup skim milk

Steps to Cook

1. Add almonds, low-fat yogurt, ice cubes, and skim milk into the blender.
2. Blend the compound until smooth.
3. Pour into the glasses and top with mint and garnish it with almond slices and serve it.
4. Enjoy!

Chapter 9: Drink and Smoothie Recipes

9.27 Chocolate Nut Smoothie

TIME TO PREPARE

5 minutes

COOK TIME

0 minutes

SERVING

2 people

Nutritional Facts

157 kcal

9 gr Prot.

Ingredients

- 1 tbsp chocolate powder
- ¼ cup nuts
- 1 banana
- 1 cup low-fat yogurt
- ½ cup ice cubes
- ⅓ cup skim milk
- Chia seeds for garnish

Steps to Cook

1. Add chocolate powder, nuts, banana, low-fat yogurt, ice cube, and skim milk into the blender.

2. Blend all ingredients until smooth.

3. Pour into the glasses and top with chia seeds and garnish it with banana slices and serve it.

4. Enjoy!

Chapter 9: Drink and Smoothie Recipes

9.28 Dates Shake

TIME TO PREPARE

5 minutes

COOK TIME

0 minutes

SERVING

2 people

Nutritional Facts

146 kcal

9 gr Prot.

Ingredients

- ½ cup dates
- Mint leaves for garnish
- 1 cup low-fat yogurt
- ½ cup ice cubes
- ½ cup skim milk

Steps to Cook

1. Add dates, low-fat yogurt, ice cubes, and skim milk into the blender.
2. Blend until smooth.
3. Pour into the glasses and top with mint and garnish it with dates slices and serve it.
4. Enjoy!

Chapter 9: Drink and Smoothie Recipes

9.29 Avocado Smoothie

TIME TO PREPARE

5 minutes

COOK TIME

0 minutes

SERVING

2 people

Nutritional Facts

137 kcal

9 gr Prot.

Ingredients

- 1 cup avocado cubes
- Mint leaves for garnish
- 1 cup low-fat yogurt
- ½ cup ice cubes
- ½ cup skim milk

Steps to Cook

1. Add avocadoes, low-fat yogurt, ice cubes, and skim milk into the blender.
2. Blend until smooth.
3. Pour into the glasses and top with mint and garnish it with avocado slices and serve it.
4. Enjoy!

Chapter 9: Drink and Smoothie Recipes

9.30 Fat-Burning Smoothie

TIME TO PREPARE

5 minutes

COOK TIME

0 minutes

SERVING

2 people

Nutritional Facts

133 kcal

9 gr Prot.

Ingredients

- 1 cup melon cubes
- ½ cup spinach leaves
- Mint leaves for garnish
- 1 cup low-fat yogurt
- ½ cup ice cubes
- ½ cup skim milk

Steps to Cook

1. Add melon, spinach leaves, low-fat yogurt, ice cubes, and skim milk into the blender.
2. Blend until smooth.
3. Pour into the glasses and top with mint and garnish it with melon slices and serve it.
4. Enjoy!

Chapter 9: Drink and Smoothie Recipes

9.31 Strawberry Protein Smoothie

TIME TO PREPARE

5 minutes

COOK TIME

0 minutes

SERVING

2 people

Nutritional Facts

133 kcal

8 gr Prot.

Ingredients

- ½ **cup** pomegranate juice
- A handful of fresh mint
- 2 cups strawberries
- 1 banana
- 1 cup low-fat yogurt
- ½ cup ice cubes

Steps to Cook

1. Add pomegranate juice, mint, strawberries, banana, and low-fat yogurt or milk into the blender.
2. Blend until smooth.
3. Pour into the glasses and top with mint. Serve.

Chapter 9: Drink and Smoothie Recipes

9.32 Peanut Butter Smoothie

TIME TO PREPARE

5 minutes

COOK TIME

0 minutes

SERVING

2 people

Nutritional Facts

135 kcal

9 gr Prot.

Ingredients

- 1 tbsp peanut butter
- 1 banana
- Mint leaves for garnish
- 1 cup low-fat yogurt
- ½ cup ice cubes
- ½ cup skim milk
- Peanuts for garnish

Steps to Cook

1. Add banana, peanut butter, low-fat yogurt, ice cubes, and skim milk into the blender.
2. Blend until smooth.
3. Pour into the glasses and top with mint and garnish it with peanuts and banana slices and serve it.
4. Enjoy!

Chapter 9: Drink and Smoothie Recipes

9.33 Blueberry Ginger Smoothie

TIME TO PREPARE

5 minutes

COOK TIME

0 minutes

SERVING

2 people

Nutritional Facts

145 kcal

8 gr Prot.

Ingredients

- 1 cup low-fat yogurt
- 2 cups frozen blueberries
- 2 tbsp freshly grated ginger
- A pinch of cinnamon
- ⅔ cup low-fat milk
- 1 tsp honey
- ½ tsp vanilla bean paste

Steps to Cook

1. In a blender, add yogurt and blueberries and puree them.

2. Now add freshly grated ginger and cinnamon and blend it out.

3. Now add low-fat milk and blend it again. If the consistency is too thick then add more low-fat milk until desired consistency is achieved.

4. Now add honey and vanilla bean paste and blend it out again until smooth.

5. Now pour the smoothie into the glasses and garnish them with blueberries. Serve and enjoy.

Chapter 9: Drink and Smoothie Recipes

9.34 Fat-Burning Watermelon Smoothie

TIME TO PREPARE

5 minutes

COOK TIME

0 minutes

SERVING

2 people

Nutritional Facts

112 kcal

8 gr Prot.

Ingredients

- 1 cup watermelon cubes
- Mint leaves for garnish
- 1 cup low-fat yogurt
- ½ cup ice cubes
- ½ cup skim milk

Steps to Cook

1. Add watermelon, low-fat yogurt, ice cubes, and skim milk into the blender.
2. Blend until smooth.
3. Pour into the glasses and top with mint and garnish it with watermelon slices and serve it.
4. Enjoy!

9.35 Matcha Smoothie

TIME TO PREPARE

5 minutes

COOK TIME

0 minutes

SERVING

2 people

Nutritional Facts

135 kcal

8 gr Prot.

Ingredients

- 1 tbsp matcha green tea
- 1 tbsp protein powder
- Mint leaves for garnish
- 1 cup low-fat yogurt
- ½ cup ice cubes
- ½ cup skim milk

Steps to Cook

1. Add matcha green tea, protein powder, low-fat yogurt, ice cubes, and skim milk into the blender.

2. Blend until smooth.

3. Pour into the glasses and top with mint and garnish it with matcha powder and serve it.

4. Enjoy!

Chapter 9: Drink and Smoothie Recipes

9.36 Cinnamon Apple Smoothie

TIME TO PREPARE

5 minutes

COOK TIME

0 minutes

SERVING

2 people

Nutritional Facts

134 kcal

8 gr Prot.

Ingredients

- 1 cup apple cubes
- 1 tsp cinnamon
- Mint leaves for garnish
- 1 cup fat-free yogurt
- ½ cup ice cubes
- ½ cup low-fat milk

Steps to Cook

1. Add apples, cinnamon, fat-free yogurt, ice cubes, and skim milk into the blender.
2. Blend until smooth.
3. Pour into the glasses and top with mint and garnish it and serve it.

Chapter 9: Drink and Smoothie Recipes

9.37 Pineapple Weight-Loss Smoothie

TIME TO PREPARE
5 minutes

COOK TIME
0 minutes

SERVING
2 people

Nutritional Facts
157 kcal
8 gr Prot.

Ingredients

- 1 cup pineapple cubes
- Mint leaves for garnish
- 1 cup low-fat yogurt
- ½ cup ice cubes
- ½ cup skim milk

Steps to Cook

1. Add pineapples, low-fat yogurt, ice cubes, and skim milk into the blender.
2. Blend until smooth.
3. Pour into the glasses and top with mint and garnish it with pineapple slices and serve it.
4. Enjoy!

Chapter 9: Drink and Smoothie Recipes

9.38 Citrus Smoothie

TIME TO PREPARE
5 minutes

COOK TIME
0 minutes

SERVING
2 people

Nutritional Facts
111 kcal
8 gr Prot.

Ingredients

- 1 cup oranges
- Mint leaves for garnish
- 6–8 almonds
- 1 tsp agave syrup
- ½ cup ice cubes
- ½ cup milk
- 1 cup fat-free yogurt

Steps to Cook

1. Add oranges, almonds, fat-free yogurt, ice cubes, skim milk, and agave syrup into the blender.
2. Blend until smooth.
3. Pour into the glasses and top with mint and garnish it with almond slices and serve it.

Chapter 9: Drink and Smoothie Recipes

9.39 Blueberry Smoothie Bowl

TIME TO PREPARE

5 minutes

COOK TIME

0 minutes

SERVING

2 people

Nutritional Facts

157 kcal

9 gr Prot.

Ingredients

- 1 cup fat-free yogurt
- 1 cup blueberries
- ¼ cup walnuts
- ¼ cup almonds
- Chia seeds for garnish

Steps to Cook

1. Take a blender and add fat-free yogurt and blueberries in it and blend it properly.
2. Take out the blueberry smoothie in a bowl and garnish it with blueberries, walnuts, almonds, and chia seeds.
3. Serve. Enjoy!

Chapter 9: Drink and Smoothie Recipes

9.40 Raspberry Chia Smoothie Bowl

TIME TO PREPARE

5 minutes

COOK TIME

0 minutes

SERVING

2 people

Nutritional Facts

137 kcal

9 gr Prot.

Ingredients

- 1 cup fat-free yogurt
- 1 cup raspberries
- ¼ cup walnuts
- ¼ cup almonds
- Chia seeds for garnish

Steps to Cook

1. Take a blender and add fat-free yogurt and raspberries in it and blend it properly.
2. Take out the raspberry smoothie in a bowl and garnish it with blueberries, walnuts, almonds, and chia seeds.
3. Serve. Enjoy!

Chapter 10:
Soups for Whole Body Reset Diet

Chapter 10: Soup Recipes

10.1 Creamy Tomato Soup

TIME TO PREPARE
5 minutes

COOK TIME
10 minutes

SERVING
4 people

Nutritional Facts
157 kcal
25 gr Prot.

Ingredients

- 4 cups tomatoes puree
- 2 tbsp olive oil
- 1 large onion , chopped
- 2 garlic cloves, minced
- 2 tbsp tomato paste
- 2 cups vegetable broth or water
- 1 cup coconut milk
- 1 tsp salt
- 1 tsp ground black pepper
- Fresh rosemary twig for garnish

Steps to Cook

1. Take a large soup pot, heat the olive oil, add onion and sauté for about 4–5 minutes until tender and translucent.
2. Then add garlic and cook for about 2 minutes, afterward add tomato paste, season with black pepper and salt and cook for 3–4 minutes until tomatoes become darker.
3. Then add tomatoes puree, coconut milk, and broth. Mix well. After it boils close the lid and cook for 25–30 minutes on medium heat. Turn off the flame and remove it.
4. Pour the soup into a bowl. Top with rosemary and serve hot with garlic bread.

Chapter 10: Soup Recipes

10.2 Chickpea Potato Soup

TIME TO PREPARE

5 minutes

COOK TIME

10 minutes

SERVING

4 people

Nutritional Facts

132 kcal

25 gr Prot.

Ingredients

- 2 tbsp olive oil
- 2 large potatoes, peeled and chopped
- 1 garlic clove, minced
- 1 tsp salt
- 1 tsp black pepper
- ½ tsp oregano
- ½ tsp thyme
- 1 onion, chopped
- 1 ½ cup chickpea, canned or cooked
- 2 cupsss vegetable broth
- 1 cup coconut milk
- Roasted chickpea and cilantro for garnish

Steps to Cook

1. In a saucepan, heat the oil, add onion and garlic, and sauté for about 1–2 minutes until translucent. Season with black pepper and salt.

2. Add chopped potatoes, chickpea, vegetable broth, and coconut milk. Mix well and close the lid.

3. Cook for about 10–15 minutes and turn off the flame. Blend well with an electric mixer.

4. Again, turn on the flame, heat, sprinkle some herbs, and remove from the stove.

5. Pour the soup into a bowl, garnish with cilantro, and top with roasted chickpeas.

6. Serve with lemon slices and warm. Enjoy!

Chapter 10: Soup Recipes

10.3 Pumpkin Soup

TIME TO PREPARE

5 minutes

COOK TIME

10 minutes

SERVING

4 people

Nutritional Facts

143 kcal

25 gr Prot.

Ingredients

- 2 cups pumpkin, cut in cubes
- 1 onion, chopped finely
- 2 garlic cloves, chopped finely
- 3 cups vegetable broth
- 1 tsp black pepper
- 1 tsp kosher salt
- 1 tbsp olive oil
- 1 tsp pumpkin seeds
- 1 tbsp fresh parsley, finely chopped
- 2 tbsp coconut milk

Steps to Cook

1. Take a large pan and add olive oil. When the oil becomes warm, add chopped onion and garlic to it. Cook for 3–5 minutes until it gets brown, then add pumpkin.

2. Gently mix the onion with pumpkin for 5–10 minutes. Add salt and black pepper. After that add 3 cups of vegetable broth, mix properly, cover the pan with a lid and wait for 10–15 minutes.

3. When the pumpkin becomes soft, whisk the soup properly or blend in a food processor until it is smooth.

4. Garnish the soup with pumpkin seed and parsley. Pour some coconut milk. Serve warm with garlic bread.

Chapter 10: Soup Recipes

10.4 Ginger Carrot Soup

TIME TO PREPARE

5 minutes

COOK TIME

10 minutes

SERVING

4 people

Nutritional Facts

134 kcal

25 gr Prot.

Ingredients

- 8 carrots, peeled and sliced
- 1 tsp salt
- 1 tsp black pepper
- 1 cup red onion, chopped
- 2 tbsp olive oil
- 4 cups vegetable broth or water
- 1 tbsp ginger, grated
- 2 garlic cloves
- Chopped dill for garnishing
- 1 tbsp apple cider vinegar

Steps to Cook

1. Take a soup pot, pour oil, and heat over medium heat. Add the onion and garlic and cook until translucent and fragrant.
2. Add carrots and cook for about 8–10 minutes. Then add ginger, season with black pepper and salt, and mix well.
3. Then add broth and vinegar and mix well. Cook for about 15–20 minutes until carrots soften. Cool and blend until smooth.
4. Pour again into the pot, warm, and serve in a soup bowl.
5. Garnish with dill and serve hot with garlic bread.

Chapter 10: Soup Recipes

10.5 Lemon Lentil Soup

TIME TO PREPARE

5 minutes

COOK TIME

10 minutes

SERVING

4 people

Nutritional Facts

134 kcal

25 gr Prot.

Ingredients

- 1 cup green and black lentils, soaked and rinsed
- ½ cup carrots, peeled, and diced
- 1 large potato, diced
- 2 tbsp olive oil
- 1 large onion, diced
- 2 garlic cloves, minced
- 4–5 cups vegetable broth
- ½ cup tomatoes, diced
- 1 tsp salt
- 1 tsp black pepper
- 1 tsp red chili powder
- 2 tbsp lemon juice and lemon slices
- Bay leaves
- Basil leaves

Steps to Cook

1. In a saucepan, warm the olive oil, add onion and sauté for 2 minutes until it becomes translucent, then add garlic and sauté until fragrant. Add potatoes and carrots and stir for 5–7 minutes.

2. Then add lentils, broth, tomatoes, salt, black pepper, chili powder, and bay leaves in it. Mix well. After simmering close the lid and cook for about 35–40 minutes until all the ingredients become softened. Stir gradually.

3. Remove the bay leaves. Blend the mixture with an electric blender to form soup consistency.

4. Add lemon juice to it and stir. Reheat the soup and ladle the soup into a bowl. Serve warm with lemon slices, sprinkled red chili powder, and top with basil leaves.

Chapter 10: Soup Recipes

10.6 Red Lentil Soup

TIME TO PREPARE

5 minutes

COOK TIME

10 minutes

SERVING

4 people

Nutritional Facts

175 kcal

25 gr Prot.

Ingredients

- 1 cup red lentils, soaked, rinsed
- 1 red onion, chopped
- 2 garlic cloves, minced
- 1 carrot, medium and diced
- 1 cup tomatoes, chopped
- 1 tbsp tomato paste
- 2 tbsp olive oil
- 1 tsp salt
- 1 tsp black pepper
- 1 tsp cumin powder
- 1 tsp cayenne
- 4 cups vegetable stock/broth
- 1 tsp lemon zest
- 4 tbsp cilantro, chopped

Steps to Cook

1. In a large pot heat, the oil. Add onion and garlic and sauté until translucent and fragrant.

2. Then add carrot, tomato paste, salt, black pepper, cumin powder, and cayenne in it and stir.

3. Add vegetable broth, lentils, and tomatoes in it and stir occasionally. Simmer for about 25–30 minutes or until lentils and carrots become soft.

4. With a hand blender, blend the mixture until it thickens, not pureed.

5. Add lemon zest and cilantro to it. Stir well. Reheat the soup and pour it into the soup bowl.

6. Garnish with some extra cilantro. Serve warm and enjoy delicious red lentil soup.

10.7 Butternut Squash Soup

TIME TO PREPARE

5 minutes

COOK TIME

10 minutes

SERVING

4 people

Nutritional Facts

133 kcal

25 gr Prot.

Ingredients

- 2 tbsp oil
- ½ cup onion, chopped
- 2 garlic cloves, minced
- 2 cups butternut squash, cut into cubes
- 3 cups milk
- 1 cup vegetable broth
- 1 tsp salt
- 1 tsp black pepper
- 1 tsp paprika
- 1 tsp oregano
- 1 tsp ginger powder
- 2 tbsp lemon juice
- 2 tbsp cilantro, chopped
- Coconut milk

Steps to Cook

1. Take a large pot and heat the oil. Add onion and sauté for about 2 minutes until translucent. Then add garlic and sauté for 15 seconds.

2. Afterward, add butternut squash cubes, milk, broth, paprika, oregano, salt, black pepper, and ginger powder and stir well.

3. After one boil simmer for 25–30 minutes or until butternut squash softens.

4. Take an immersion blender and blend until all the mixture well combines and thickens. Reheat the soup and stir in cilantro and lemon juice.

5. Pour the warm soup into a bowl. Garnish with fresh cilantro and coconut milk so it looks captivating.

Chapter 10: Soup Recipes

10.8 Creamy Asparagus Soup

TIME TO PREPARE

5 minutes

COOK TIME

10 minutes

SERVING

4 people

Nutritional Facts

164 kcal

27 gr Prot.

Ingredients

- 1 pound asparagus, trimmed and cut into pieces
- 1 potato, cubed
- 1 onion, chopped
- 2 garlic cloves, minced
- 1 tsp ginger, grated
- 2 tbsp olive oil
- 1 tsp kosher salt
- 1 tsp black pepper
- 3 cups vegetable broth
- 2 cups full-fat coconut milk
- 1 tsp thyme, freshly chopped
- 1 tsp dill, chopped
- ¼ cup cashew, grounded

Steps to Cook

1. In a large pot heat, the oil. Add onion and sauté until translucent but not browned. Then add garlic and ginger and sauté until fragrant.

2. Add asparagus, potato, salt, and black pepper and stir for 2–4 minutes. Afterward, add herbs like thyme and dill. Stir well.

3. Then add cashew, broth, and coconut milk. Bring to boil and simmer for 25–30 minutes or until vegetables become soft.

4. Turn off the flame. Take an immersion blender and blend the compound until it becomes thick and smooth.

5. Reheat the soup and pour it into a soup bowl.

6. Top with baked asparagus. Serve with garlic toast and enjoy.

Chapter 10: Soup Recipes

10.9 Sweet Potato Soup

TIME TO PREPARE

5 minutes

COOK TIME

10 minutes

SERVING

4 people

Nutritional Facts

144 kcal

25 gr Prot.

Ingredients

- 3 cups sweet potato, peeled and diced
- 2 carrots, peeled and diced
- 1 tsp salt
- 1 tsp black pepper
- 1 tsp thyme
- 1 tsp oregano
- 1 tsp dill, dried
- 1 cup red onion, chopped
- 2 tbsp olive oil
- 4 cups vegetable broth or water
- 1 cup coconut milk
- 1 tbsp ginger, grated
- 2 garlic cloves
- 1 tbsp lime juice
- Coconut milk and cilantro to garnish
- Croutons

Steps to Cook

1. Take a saucepan and heat the oil. Add onion and carrots and stir until carrots become soft. Then add ginger and garlic and sauté for about 5–8 minutes.
2. Then add sweet potato, season with black pepper and salt, and add herbs like thyme, oregano, and dill. Stir continuously.
3. Add vegetable broth and coconut milk and when it starts boiling slow the flame. Simmer for about 25–30 minutes until vegetables are soft.
4. Turn off the flame. Blend with an immersion blender. Reheat and add lime juice. Stir well.
5. Pour into the bowl and garnish with coconut milk and cilantro.
6. Serve warm with croutons. Enjoy!

Chapter 10: Soup Recipes

10.10 Spinach Soup

TIME TO PREPARE

5 minutes

COOK TIME

10 minutes

SERVING

4 people

Nutritional Facts

146 kcal

25 gr Prot.

Ingredients

- 1 cup puree spinach
- 2 cups vegetable stock
- Salt to taste
- 1 tsp black pepper
- 1 tsp vinegar
- 1 tsp soy sauce
- 1 tsp chili sauce
- 2 tsp cornflour
- ½ cup low-fat cream

Steps to Cook

1. First, pour the vegetable stock and spinach puree into a pan and cook them on medium heat.

2. Add salt, black pepper, vinegar, soy sauce, and chili sauce, and cook it on medium heat for 20 minutes. Now add low-fat cream to the soup and mix it well.

3. Take a bowl and add cornflour and water.

4. Add this cornflour gradually to the soup until it thickens and serve it hot.

Chapter 10: Soup Recipes

10.11 Vegetable Soup

TIME TO PREPARE

5 minutes

COOK TIME

10 minutes

SERVING

4 people

Nutritional Facts

132 kcal

25 gr Prot.

Ingredients

- 1 chopped capsicum
- 2 cups vegetable stock
- Salt to taste
- 1 tsp black pepper
- 1 tsp vinegar
- 1 tsp soy sauce
- 1 tsp chili sauce
- 2 tsp cornflour
- 1 chopped carrot
- 1 chopped onion
- 1 chopped cabbage

Steps to Cook

1. First, pour the vegetable stock into a pan and cook it on medium heat.

2. Then add capsicum, carrot, onion, cabbage, salt, black pepper, vinegar, soy sauce, and chili sauce and cook it on medium heat for 20 minutes.

3. Take a bowl and add cornflour and water.

4. Add this cornflour gradually to the soup until it thickens and serve it hot.

Chapter 10: Soup Recipes

10.12 Creamy Whole Wheat Pasta Soup

TIME TO PREPARE

5 minutes

COOK TIME

10 minutes

SERVING

4 people

Nutritional Facts

167 kcal

25 gr Prot.

Ingredients

- 4 cups vegetable stock
- 1 cup boiled pasta
- 1 tbsp butter
- 1 tbsp chopped garlic
- 2 tbsp chopped onion
- 2 tbsp chopped carrots
- 2 tbsp peas
- 1 tsp salt
- 1 tsp dried thyme
- 1 tsp pepper
- 1 cup low-fat milk
- ½ cup cream
- 2 tbsp corn flour

Steps to Cook

1. In a large cooking pot, add butter, onions, and garlic, and sauté them for 1 minute.

2. Then add pasta, carrots, and peas, and let it cook for one more minute. Afterward, add prepared vegetable stock and bring it to boil.

3. Now add salt, pepper, and thyme and give it a good mix. Finally, add cream and cornflour dissolved in low-fat milk and stir the mixture slowly.

4. Now let the soup simmer for 2 minutes and it is ready to serve.

Chapter 10: Soup Recipes

10.13 French Onion Soup

TIME TO PREPARE
5 minutes

COOK TIME
10 minutes

SERVING
4 people

Nutritional Facts
135 kcal
25 gr Prot.

Ingredients

- 1 large onion
- ¼ cup vegetable stock
- 1 tbsp butter
- 1 tsp garlic powder
- 1 tsp sugar
- 4 cups water
- 1 tsp salt
- 1 tsp pepper
- 1 tbsp flour
- ½ cup low-fat cheese
- 2 bread slices

Steps to Cook

1. In a cooking pot, add butter and onion and sauté them until translucent. Then add flour and give it a good mix.

2. Now add vegetable stock, sugar, and water and cook it on low flame for 30 minutes.

3. Now add garlic powder, salt, pepper, and low-fat cheese and cook it until the cheese melts.

4. Now add soup to 2 bowls and put bread slices on top. Now add the remaining vegan cheese on top and broil it for 3 minutes. French onion soup is ready to serve.

Chapter 10: Soup Recipes

10.14 Roasted Carrot Soup

TIME TO PREPARE

5 minutes

COOK TIME

10 minutes

SERVING

4 people

Nutritional Facts

165 kcal

27 gr Prot.

Ingredients

- 2 cups roasted carrots
- 2 cups vegetable broth
- ½ medium onion
- 1 garlic clove, minced
- 1 tsp salt
- 1 tsp pepper
- 1 tsp dried thyme
- 1 tbsp olive oil
- 1 tsp ground cumin
- 1 tsp dried coriander

Steps to Cook

1. In a cooking pot, add olive oil, onion, and garlic and sauté them Until translucent.
2. Then, add vegetable broth, salt, pepper, and ground cumin and bring it to a boil.
3. Now add roasted carrots and remove the pot from heat. Now blend the soup with the help of a hand blender until smooth.
4. Afterward, simmer the blended soup for 3 minutes and add dried thyme and coriander. Now serve the soup hot in the bowls.

Chapter 10: Soup Recipes

10.15 Red Bean Soup

TIME TO PREPARE
5 minutes

COOK TIME
10 minutes

SERVING
4 people

Nutritional Facts
175 kcal
27 gr Prot.

Ingredients

- 1 ½ cup red beans, soaked and drained
- 2 tbsp olive oil
- 1 onion, chopped
- 2 garlic cloves, minced
- 1 celery, chopped
- 5 cups vegetable broth
- 1 tsp salt
- 1 tsp black pepper
- 1 tsp cumin powder
- ½ tsp oregano
- ½ tsp dried rosemary
- 2 bay leaves
- 1 tbsp lime juice, fresh
- 2 tbsp parsley, chopped

Steps to Cook

1. Heat oil in a pan and sauté onion. Then add garlic and stir frequently until fragrant.

2. Add red beans, celery, vegetable broth, salt, black pepper, cumin powder, oregano, rosemary, and bay leaves. Stir occasionally. When it starts to simmer close the lid and cook f o r about 35–40 minutes.

3. Remove the bay leaves, blend half the mixture with an electric blender and mix with the other half to make a thick consistency, not a puree. Cook for another 2–3 minutes to warmup.

4. Add parsley and lime juice and stir. Pour the soup into a bowl.

5. Serve warm. Enjoy!

Chapter 10: Soup Recipes

10.16 Cauliflower Soup

TIME TO PREPARE

5 minutes

COOK TIME

10 minutes

SERVING

4 people

Nutritional Facts

144 kcal

27 gr Prot.

Ingredients

- 1 chopped large head of cauliflower
- 1 chopped red onion
- 2 minced garlic cloves
- 1 tbsp olive oil
- 2 small potatoes, chopped
- 1 tsp salt
- 2 tsp grounded black pepper
- 1 tbsp chopped fresh rosemary
- 1 tbsp chopped fresh dill
- 1 tsp cayenne powder
- 4 cups vegetable broth
- 1 tbsp cornflour

Steps to Cook

1. Take a saucepan, heat the oil, and add onion and sauté for 2–3 minutes. Then add garlic and sauté until fragrant.
2. Add cauliflower, potatoes, black pepper, salt, fresh rosemary, dill, and cayenne powder. Stir rarely.
3. Then add vegetable broth and simmer for about 25–30 minutes until the vegetables are tender.
4. In a bowl, mix cornflour with water and pour in the soup. Stir gently.
5. With a hand blender, blend half the mixture and pour it into the other half. Reheat the soup if required. Ladle the soup in a serving soup bowl.
6. Garnish with fresh cilantro and sprinkle some black pepper.

Chapter 10: Soup Recipes

10.17 Creamy Mushroom Soup

TIME TO PREPARE
5 minutes

COOK TIME
10 minutes

SERVING
4 people

Nutritional Facts
134 kcal
20 gr Prot.

Ingredients

- 2 tbsp coconut oil
- 1 chopped onion
- 2 minced garlic cloves
- 2 cups mushrooms, thinly sliced
- 2 cups coconut milk
- 2 cups vegetable broth
- 1 tsp paprika
- 1 tsp salt
- 1 tsp black pepper
- 1 tsp oregano
- 1 tbsp chopped dill
- 2 tbsp coconut flour
- Cilantro and mushrooms for topping

Steps to Cook

1. In a saucepan, melt the oil. Add onion and garlic and sauté for 2–3 minutes until translucent and fragrant.
2. Then add mushrooms and stir occasionally until the mushrooms' color change.
3. Then add paprika, black pepper, salt, oregano, and dill. Stir well. Pour broth and coconut milk in it and mix. Cook for about 20–25 minutes.
4. In a separate bowl mix coconut flour with coconut milk. Pour the mixture into the soup and stir. Add more coconut flour to reach the desired consistency.
5. Ladle the soup in a bowl. Garnish with mushrooms, black pepper, and cilantro.
6. Serve warm with gingerbread and enjoy.

Chapter 10: Soup Recipes

10.18 Broccoli Soup

TIME TO PREPARE

5 minutes

COOK TIME

10 minutes

SERVING

4 people

Nutritional Facts

134 kcal

20 gr Prot.

Ingredients

- 2 cups of roughly chopped fresh broccoli
- 1 cup chickpea, soaked and rinsed
- 1 diced potato
- 2 cups vegetable broth
- 2 cups coconut milk
- 1 chopped onion
- 2 chopped garlic cloves
- 2 tbsp olive oil
- 1 tsp salt
- 1 tsp black pepper
- 1 tsp oregano
- 1 tsp thyme
- 1 tsp rosemary

Steps to Cook

1. Take a large soup pot, heat the oil, add onion and garlic, and sauté for 2–3 minutes until translucent and fragrant.
2. Add broccoli, potato, and chickpea. Stir frequently. Then add vegetable broth and coconut milk and season with black pepper, salt, oregano, thyme, and rosemary. Stir well.
3. Simmer for about 20–25 minutes until all the ingredients get a soft consistency. Blend the mixture with an electric blender.
4. Reheat the soup and pour it into the bowl. Sprinkle some more salt and black pepper according to taste.
5. Serve warm with almond garlic bread. Enjoy!

Chapter 10: Soup Recipes

10.19 Hot and Sour Soup

TIME TO PREPARE

5 minutes

COOK TIME

10 minutes

SERVING

4 people

Nutritional Facts

157 kcal

25 gr Prot.

Ingredients

- 2 cups chicken stock
- 1 cup boiled and shredded chicken
- ½ cup chopped capsicum
- ½ cup chopped carrot
- ½ cup chopped cabbage
- 1 tbsp cornflour
- Salt to taste
- 1 tbsp black pepper
- 1 tbsp soy sauce
- 1 tbsp chili sauce
- 1 tsp vinegar

Steps to Cook

1. Take a saucepan and add chicken stock, shredded chicken, chopped capsicum, carrot, and cabbage in it. Mix it very well.

2. Boil it for 10 minutes and then add salt, black pepper, soy sauce, chili

   sauce, and vinegar in it. Mix it very well.

3. Take a small bowl and cornflour and some water in it. Mix it.

4. Pour a mixture of cornflour and water into the soup and mix it till the soup becomes thick, add more cornflower if required.

5. Take out chicken hot and sour soup in a soup bowl and serve it hot. Enjoy!

Chapter 10: Soup Recipes

10.20 Chicken Corn Soup

TIME TO PREPARE

5 minutes

COOK TIME

10 minutes

SERVING

4 people

Nutritional Facts

134 kcal

25 gr Prot.

Ingredients

- 2 cups chicken stock
- 1 cup boiled and shredded chicken
- ½ cup boiled corns
- 1 tbsp cornflour
- Salt to taste
- 1 tbsp black pepper
- 1 tsp soy sauce

Steps to Cook

1. Take a saucepan and add chicken stock, shredded chicken, and boiled corns. Mix it very well.
2. Boil it for 10 minutes and then add salt, black pepper, and soy sauce. Mix it very well.
3. Take a small bowl and cornflour and some water in it. Mix it.
4. Pour this cornflour mixture into the soup and mix it till the soup becomes thick, add more cornflower if required.
5. Take out chicken and the corn soup in a soup bowl and serve it hot. Enjoy!

Chapter 10: Soup Recipes

10.21 Kale and Bean Soup

TIME TO PREPARE

5 minutes

COOK TIME

10 minutes

SERVING

4 people

Nutritional Facts

157 kcal

20 gr Prot.

Ingredients

- 4 cups chicken stock
- 1 tbsp cornflour
- Salt to taste
- 1 tbsp black pepper
- 1 tbsp vinegar
- 1 tbsp chili sauce
- 1 tbsp soy sauce
- 1 cup beans
- 1 cup kale
- 1 tbsp oregano
- ¼ cup carrot cubes
- ¼ cup capsicum cubes
- ¼ cup boiled potatoes cubes
- ¼ cup cabbage cubes

Steps to Cook

1. First, take a small bowl and add cornflour and water. Mix it very well to form a paste. Put it aside.

2. Then take a saucepan and add chicken stock, kale, beans, carrot, capsicum, boiled potatoes cubes, and cabbage. Mix it very well. Boil it for 10 minutes.

3. Then add salt, black pepper, oregano, chili sauce, soy sauce, and vinegar in it. Mix it very well.

4. Then pour cornflour paste into it. Mix it till the soup becomes thick.

5. Then pour kale and bean soup into a soup bowl.

6. Serve it hot. Enjoy!

Chapter 10: Soup Recipes

10.22 Potato Soup

TIME TO PREPARE

5 minutes

COOK TIME

10 minutes

SERVING

4 people

Nutritional Facts

127 kcal

20 gr Prot.

Ingredients

- 1 lb peeled potatoes, chopped
- 1 chopped red onion
- 2 minced garlic cloves
- 1 tbsp olive oil
- 1 tsp salt
- 2 tsp grounded black pepper
- 1 tbsp chopped fresh rosemary
- 1 tbsp chopped fresh dill
- 1 tsp cayenne powder
- 4 cups vegetable broth
- 1 tbsp cornflour

Steps to Cook

1. Take a saucepan, heat the oil, and add onion and sauté for 2–3 minutes. Then add garlic and sauté until fragrant.

2. Add potatoes, black pepper, salt, fresh rosemary, dill, and cayenne powder. Stir rarely.

3. Then add vegetable broth in it and simmer for about 25–30 minutes until the vegetables are tender.

4. In a bowl, mix cornflour with water and pour in the soup. Stir gently.

5. With a hand blender, blend half the mixture and pour it into the other half. Reheat the soup if required. Ladle the soup in a serving soup bowl.

6. Garnish with fresh cilantro and sprinkle some black pepper. Serve it hot. Enjoy!

Chapter 10: Soup Recipes

10.23 Parsnip Pear Soup

TIME TO PREPARE

5 minutes

COOK TIME

10 minutes

SERVING

4 people

Nutritional Facts

135 kcal

20 gr Prot.

Ingredients

- 1 lb parsnip
- 1 pear
- 1 chopped red onion
- 2 minced garlic cloves
- 1 tbsp olive oil
- 1 tsp salt
- 2 tsp grounded black pepper
- 1 tbsp chopped fresh rosemary
- 1 tbsp chopped fresh dill
- 1 tsp cayenne powder
- 4 cups vegetable broth
- 1 tbsp cornflour

Steps to Cook

1. Take a saucepan, heat the oil, add onion, and sauté for 2–3 minutes. Then add garlic and sauté until fragrant.

2. Add parsnip, pear, black pepper, salt, fresh rosemary, dill, and cayenne powder. Stir rarely.

3. Then add vegetable broth in it and simmer for about 25–30 minutes until the vegetables become tender.

4. In a bowl mix cornflour with water and pour in the soup. Stir gently.

5. With a hand blender, blend half the mixture and pour it into the other half. Reheat the soup if required. Ladle the soup in a serving soup bowl.

6. Garnish with fresh cilantro and sprinkle some black pepper. Serve it hot. Enjoy!

Chapter 10: Soup Recipes

10.24 Tuscany Protein Soup

TIME TO PREPARE

5 minutes

COOK TIME

10 minutes

SERVING

4 people

Nutritional Facts

177 kcal

25 gr Prot.

Ingredients	Steps to Cook

Ingredients

- 4 cups chicken stock
- 1 tbsp cornflour
- Salt to taste
- 1 tbsp black pepper
- 1 tbsp vinegar
- 1 tbsp chili sauce
- 1 tbsp soy sauce
- 1 chicken breast, cut into slices
- 1 tbsp oregano
- ¼ cup carrot cubes
- ¼ cup capsicum cubes
- ¼ cup boiled potatoes cubes
- ¼ cup cabbage cubes

Steps to Cook

1. First, take a small bowl and add cornflour and water. Mix it very well to form a paste. Put it aside.
2. Then take a saucepan and add chicken stock, chicken pieces, carrot, capsicum, boiled potatoes cubes, and cabbage. Mix it very well. Boil it for 10 minutes.
3. Then add salt, black pepper, oregano, chili sauce, soy sauce, and vinegar. Mix it very well.
4. Then pour the cornflour paste. Mix it till the soup become thickens.
5. Then pour the Tuscany protein soup into a soup bowl.
6. Serve it hot. Enjoy!

Chapter 10: Soup Recipes

10.25 Low-Fat Beef Soup

TIME TO PREPARE
5 minutes

COOK TIME
20 minutes

SERVING
4 people

Nutritional Facts
145 kcal
30 gr Prot.

Ingredients

- 4 cups chicken stock
- 1 tbsp cornflour
- Salt to taste
- 1 tbsp black pepper
- 1 tbsp vinegar
- 1 tbsp chili sauce
- 1 tbsp soy sauce
- 1 lb beef cubes (without fat)
- 1 tbsp oregano
- ¼ cup carrot cubes
- ¼ cup capsicum cubes
- ¼ cup boiled potatoes cubes

Steps to Cook

1. First, take a small bowl and add cornflour and water. Mix it very well to form a paste. Put it aside.

2. Then take a saucepan and add chicken stock, beef pieces, carrot, capsicum, and boiled potato cubes in it. Mix it very well. Boil it for 10 minutes.

3. Then add salt, black pepper, oregano, chili sauce, soy sauce, and vinegar in it. Mix it very well.

4. Then pour cornflour paste. Mix it till the soup becomes thick.

5. Then pour low-fat beef soup into a soup bowl.

6. Serve it hot. Enjoy!

Chapter 10: Soup Recipes

10.26 Instant Pot Minestrone Soup

TIME TO PREPARE
5 minutes

COOK TIME
20 minutes

SERVING
4 people

Nutritional Facts
167 kcal
25 gr Prot.

Ingredients

- 4 cups chicken stock
- 1 tbsp cornflour
- Salt to taste
- 1 tbsp black pepper
- 1 tbsp vinegar
- 1 tbsp chili sauce
- 1 tbsp soy sauce
- 1 lb beef cubes
- ¼ cup onion slices
- ¼ cup peas
- 1 tbsp oregano
- ¼ cup carrot cubes
- ¼ cup capsicum cubes
- ¼ cup boiled potato cubes
- ¼ cup cabbage cubes

Steps to Cook

1. First, take a small bowl and add cornflour and water. Mix it very well to form a paste. Put it aside.
2. Then take a saucepan and add chicken stock, beef pieces, peas, onion slices, carrot, capsicum, boiled potato cubes, and cabbage. Mix it properly. Boil it for 10 minutes.
3. Then add salt, black pepper, oregano, chili sauce, soy sauce, and vinegar. Mix it properly.
4. Then pour cornflour paste. Mix it till the soup becomes thick.
5. Then pour the instant pot minestrone soup into a soup bowl.
6. Serve it hot. Enjoy!

Chapter 10: Soup Recipes

10.27 Lentil Quinoa Soup

TIME TO PREPARE

5 minutes

COOK TIME

10 minutes

SERVING

4 people

Nutritional Facts

156 kcal

30 gr Prot.

Ingredients

- 4 cups chicken stock
- 1 tbsp cornflour
- Salt to taste
- 1 tbsp black pepper
- 1 tbsp vinegar
- 1 tbsp chili sauce
- 1 tbsp soy sauce
- 2 cups lentils
- 1 tbsp oregano
- ¼ cup carrot cubes
- ¼ cup capsicum cubes
- 1 cup quinoa

Steps to Cook

1. First, take a small bowl and add cornflour and water. Mix it properly to form a paste. Put it aside.

2. Then take a saucepan and add chicken stock, lentils, quinoa, carrot, and capsicum. Mix it properly. Boil it for 10 minutes.

3. Then add salt, black pepper, oregano, chili sauce, soy sauce, and vinegar. Mix it properly.

4. Then pour cornflour paste. Mix it till the soup becomes thick.

5. Then pour lentil quinoa soup into a soup bowl.

6. Serve it hot. Enjoy!

10.28 Thai Coconut Soup

TIME TO PREPARE

5 minutes

COOK TIME

10 minutes

SERVING

4 people

Nutritional Facts

156 kcal

25 gr Prot.

Ingredients

- 4 cups of chicken stock
- 1 tbsp cornflour
- Salt to taste
- 1 tbsp black pepper
- 1 tbsp vinegar
- 1 tbsp Thai sauce
- 1 cup coconut milk
- 1 tbsp chili sauce
- 1 tbsp soy sauce
- 1 cup tofu
- 1 tbsp paprika
- 1 tbsp oregano
- ¼ cup carrot cubes
- ¼ cup capsicum cubes
- ¼ cup broccoli
- Cabbage

Steps to Cook

1. First, take a small bowl and add cornflour and water. Mix it properly to form a paste. Put it aside.
2. Then take a saucepan and add chicken stock, tofu, broccoli, carrot, capsicum, and cabbage. Mix it properly. Boil it for 10 minutes.
3. Then add salt, black pepper, oregano, paprika, chili sauce, Thai sauce, coconut milk, soy sauce, and vinegar. Mix it properly.
4. Then pour cornflour paste into it. Mix it till the soup becomes thick.
5. Then pour Thai coconut soup into a soup bowl.
6. Serve it hot. Enjoy!

10.29 Zucchini Soup

TIME TO PREPARE
5 minutes

COOK TIME
10 minutes

SERVING
4 people

Nutritional Facts
168 kcal
20 gr Prot.

Ingredients

- 1 lb zucchini
- 1 chopped red onion
- 2 minced garlic cloves
- 1 tbsp olive oil
- 1 tsp salt
- 2 tsp grounded black pepper
- 1 tbsp chopped fresh rosemary
- 1 tbsp chopped fresh dill
- 1 tsp cayenne powder
- 4 cups vegetable broth
- 1 tbsp cornflour

Steps to Cook

1. Take a saucepan, heat the oil, add onion, and sauté for 2–3 minutes. Then add garlic and sauté until fragrant.
2. Add zucchini, black pepper, salt, fresh rosemary, dill, and cayenne powder. Stir rarely.
3. Then add vegetable broth and cook for about 25–30 minutes or until vegetables become tender.
4. In a bowl mix cornflour with water and pour in the soup. Stir gently.
5. With a hand blender, blend half the mixture and pour it into the other half. Reheat the soup if required. Ladle the soup in a serving soup bowl.
6. Garnish with fresh cilantro and sprinkle some black pepper. Serve it hot. Enjoy!

Chapter 10: Soup Recipes

10.30 Chicken Carrot Soup

TIME TO PREPARE

5 minutes

COOK TIME

10 minutes

SERVING

4 people

Nutritional Facts

154 kcal

27 gr Prot.

Ingredients

- 4 cups chicken stock
- 1 tbsp cornflour
- Salt to taste
- 1 tbsp black pepper
- 1 tbsp vinegar
- 1 tbsp chili sauce
- 1 tbsp soy sauce
- 1 chicken breast, cut into slices
- 1 tbsp oregano
- ¼ cup carrot cubes

Steps to Cook

1. First, take a small bowl and add cornflour and water. Mix it properly to form a paste. Put it aside.

2. Then take a saucepan and add chicken stock, chicken pieces, and carrots. Mix it properly. Boil it for 10 minutes.

3. Then add salt, black pepper, oregano, chili sauce, soy sauce, and vinegar in it. Mix it properly.

4. Then pour cornflour paste into it. Mix it till the soup becomes thick.

5. Then pour chicken carrot soup into a soup bowl.

6. Serve it hot. Enjoy!

Chapter 10: Soup Recipes

10.31 Body Reset Egg Soup

TIME TO PREPARE

5 minutes

COOK TIME

10 minutes

SERVING

4 people

Nutritional Facts

127 kcal

25 gr Prot.

Ingredients

- 4 cups chicken stock
- 1 tbsp cornflour
- Salt to taste
- 1 tbsp black pepper
- 1 tbsp vinegar
- 1 tbsp chili sauce
- 1 tbsp soy sauce
- 1 chicken breast, cut into slices
- 1 tbsp oregano
- ¼ cup chopped asparagus
- 1 cup noodles
- 2 boiled eggs

Steps to Cook

1. First, take a small bowl and add cornflour and water. Mix it properly to form a paste. Put it aside.

2. Then take a saucepan and add chicken stock, chicken pieces, chopped asparagus, and noodles. Mix it properly. Boil it for 10 minutes.

3. Then add salt, black pepper, oregano, chili sauce, soy sauce, and vinegar in it. Mix it properly.

4. Then pour cornflour paste into it. Mix it till the soup becomes thick.

5. Then pour the egg soup into a soup bowl. Add boiled eggs on top.

6. Serve it hot. Enjoy!

Chapter 10: Soup Recipes

10.32 Chicken Clear Soup

TIME TO PREPARE

5 minutes

SERVING

4 people

Nutritional Facts

117 kcal

20 gr Prot.

COOK TIME

10 minutes

Ingredients

- Bones and carcass of 1 chicken
- 12 cups water
- 2 tbsp apple cider vinegar
- Salt and black pepper to taste
- Rosemary optional
- 1 lemon sliced

Steps to Cook

1. To a large pot, add bones, carcass, and water until the pot is fully covered. Season with salt and black pepper.

2. Then add the apple cider vinegar. Bring all the ingredients to a boil, then reduce the flame to a simmer and cover. Cook for at least 10–12 hours.

3. Strain and discard the bones. Strain the soup. Add rosemary and lemon slices. Serve it hot. Enjoy!

Chapter 10: Soup Recipes

10.33 Thai Shrimp Soup

TIME TO PREPARE
5 minutes

COOK TIME
10 minutes

SERVING
4 people

Nutritional Facts
137 kcal
27 gr Prot.

Ingredients

- 4 cups chicken stock
- 1 tbsp cornflour
- Salt to taste
- 1 tbsp black pepper
- 1 tbsp vinegar
- 1 tbsp Thai sauce
- 1 cup coconut milk
- 1 tbsp chili sauce
- 1 tbsp soy sauce
- 1 lb shrimps
- 1 tbsp paprika
- 1 tbsp oregano
- ¼ cup carrot cubes
- ¼ cup capsicum cubes
- ¼ cup broccoli
- Cabbage

Steps to Cook

1. First, take a small bowl and add cornflour and water. Mix it properly to form a paste. Put it aside.
2. Then take a saucepan and add chicken stock, shrimps, broccoli, carrot, capsicum, and cabbage. Mix it properly. Boil it for 10 minutes.
3. Then add salt, black pepper, oregano, paprika, chili sauce, Thai sauce, coconut milk, soy sauce, and vinegar in it. Mix it properly.
4. Then pour cornflour paste. Mix it till the soup becomes thick.
5. Then pour Thai shrimp soup into a soup bowl.
6. Serve it hot. Enjoy!

10.34 Ultimate Detox Soup

TIME TO PREPARE

5 minutes

COOK TIME

10 minutes

SERVING

4 people

Nutritional Facts

145 kcal

20 gr Prot.

Ingredients

- 4 cups chicken stock
- 1 tbsp cornflour
- Salt to taste
- 1 tbsp black pepper
- 1 tbsp vinegar
- 1 tbsp chili sauce
- 1 tbsp soy sauce
- 1 tbsp oregano
- ¼ cup carrot cubes
- ¼ cup capsicum cubes
- ¼ cup boiled potatoes cubes
- ¼ cup cabbage cubes
- ¼ cup spinach

Steps to Cook

1. First, take a small bowl and add cornflour and water. Mix it properly to form a paste. Put it aside.
2. Then take a saucepan and add chicken stock, carrot, capsicum, boiled potatoes cubes, spinach, and cabbage. Mix it properly. Boil it for 10 minutes.
3. Then add salt, black pepper, oregano, chili sauce, soy sauce, and vinegar. Mix it properly.
4. Then pour cornflour paste. Mix it till the soup becomes thick.
5. Then pour Ultimate Detox Soup into a soup bowl.
6. Serve it hot. Enjoy!

Chapter 10: Soup Recipes

10.35 Pea Soup

TIME TO PREPARE
5 minutes

COOK TIME
10 minutes

SERVING
4 people

Nutritional Facts
137 kcal
20 gr Prot.

Ingredients

- 1 cup peas
- 1 chopped red onion
- 2 minced garlic cloves
- 1 tbsp olive oil
- 1 tsp salt
- 2 tsp grounded black pepper
- 1 tbsp chopped fresh rosemary
- 1 tbsp chopped fresh dill
- 1 tsp cayenne powder
- 4 cups vegetable broth
- 1 tbsp cornflour

Steps to Cook

1. Take a saucepan, heat the oil, add onion, and sauté for 2–3 minutes. Then add garlic and sauté until fragrant.

2. Add peas, black pepper, salt, fresh rosemary, dill, and cayenne powder. Stir rarely.

3. Then add vegetable broth and cook for about 25–30 minutes until vegetables become tender.

4. In a bowl, mix cornflour with water and pour in the soup. Stir gently.

5. With a hand blender, blend half the mixture and pour it into the other half. Reheat the soup if required. Ladle the soup in a serving soup bowl.

6. Garnish with fresh cilantro and sprinkle some black pepper. Serve it hot. Enjoy!

10.36 Low-Fat Oxtail Soup

TIME TO PREPARE

5 minutes

COOK TIME

10 minutes

SERVING

4 people

Nutritional Facts

153 kcal

25 gr Prot.

Ingredients

- 2 lb oxtail bones
- 4 carrots chopped
- 2 onions, cubed
- 5–6 garlic cloves
- 6 stalks celery chopped
- 4 bay leaves
- ¼ cup black peppercorns
- 4 whole star anise
- 2 whole cinnamon sticks
- 2 tbsp apple cider vinegar

Steps to Cook

1. Bring oxtail bones to a boil over high heat and cook for 15–20 minutes.
2. Transfer the bones and vegetables (carrots, onions, garlic, celery) to the roasting pans. Roast for 30 minutes.
3. Transfer the bones and vegetables back to the stockpots.
4. Add the other ingredients including peppercorns, star anise, bay leaves, cinnamon sticks, and apple cider vinegar and water until bones are fully submerged. Cover the pots and bring to a boil.
5. Cook for at least 8–12 hours.
6. Skim the fat from your broth (optional).
7. Serve low-fat oxtail soup hot. Enjoy!

Chapter 10: Soup Recipes

10.37 Cabbage Soup

**TIME TO
PREPARE**

5 minutes

**COOK
TIME**

10 minutes

SERVING

4 people

**Nutritional
Facts**

111 kcal

20 gr Prot.

Ingredients

- 4 cups vegetable stock
- Salt to taste
- 1 tbsp black pepper
- 1 tbsp vinegar
- 1 tbsp chili sauce
- 1 tbsp soy sauce
- 1 tbsp oregano
- ¼ cup carrot cubes
- ¼ cup capsicum cubes
- ¼ cup cabbage cubes

Steps to Cook

1. Take a saucepan and add vegetable stock, carrot, capsicum, and cabbage in it. Mix it properly. Boil it for 10 minutes.

2. Then add salt, black pepper, oregano, chili sauce, soy sauce, and vinegar in it. Mix it properly.

3. Mix it till the soup becomes thick.

4. Then pour the cabbage soup into a soup bowl.

5. Serve it hot. Enjoy!

Chapter 10: Soup Recipes

10.38 Chicken Chowder Soup

TIME TO PREPARE
5 minutes

COOK TIME
10 minutes

SERVING
4 people

Nutritional Facts
167 kcal
27 gr Prot.

Ingredients

- 4 cups chicken stock
- 1 tbsp cornflour
- Salt to taste
- 1 tbsp black pepper
- 1 tbsp vinegar
- 1 cup coconut milk
- 1 tbsp chili sauce
- 1 tbsp soy sauce
- 1 cup boiled chicken
- ¼ cup boiled corns
- 1 tbsp paprika
- 1 tbsp oregano
- ¼ cup carrot cubes
- ¼ cup capsicum cubes
- ¼ cup broccoli
- Low-fat cream
- Cabbage

Steps to Cook

1. First, take a small bowl and add cornflour and water. Mix it properly to form a paste. Put it aside.
2. Then take a saucepan and add chicken stock, low-fat cream, boiled chicken, corns, broccoli, carrot, capsicum, and cabbage in it. Mix it properly. Boil it for 10 minutes.
3. Then add salt, black pepper, oregano, paprika, chili sauce, coconut milk, soy sauce, and vinegar in it. Mix it properly.
4. Then pour cornflour paste into it. Mix it till the soup becomes thick.
5. Then pour the chicken chowder soup into a soup bowl.
6. Serve it hot. Enjoy!

10.39 Fish Soup

TIME TO PREPARE

5 minutes

COOK TIME

10 minutes

SERVING

4 people

Nutritional Facts

154 kcal

27 gr Prot.

Ingredients

- 4 cups stock
- 1 tbsp cornflour
- Salt to taste
- 1 tbsp black pepper
- 1 tbsp vinegar
- 1 tbsp chili sauce
- 1 tbsp soy sauce
- 1 lb fish cubes
- 1 tbsp oregano
- ¼ cup carrot cubes
- ¼ cup capsicum cubes
- ¼ cup cabbage cubes

Steps to Cook

1. First, take a small bowl and add cornflour and water. Mix it properly to form a paste. Put it aside.

2. Then take a saucepan and add stock, fish pieces, carrot, capsicum, and cabbage in it. Mix it properly. Boil it for 10 minutes.

3. Then add salt, black pepper, oregano, chili sauce, soy sauce, and vinegar in it. Mix it properly.

4. Then pour cornflour paste into it. Mix it till the soup becomes thick.

5. Then pour the fish soup into a soup bowl.

6. Serve it hot. Enjoy!

Chapter 10: Soup Recipes

Chapter 11:
Salads for Whole Body Reset Diet

Chapter 11: Salad Recipes

11.1 Chicken Tomato Salad

TIME TO PREPARE

10 minutes

COOK TIME

0 minutes

SERVING

4 people

Nutritional Facts

117 kcal

20 gr Prot.

Ingredients

- 1 large bunch of lettuce
- 1 cup cherry tomatoes, halved
- ¾ cup black olives, cut into halves
- 2 red onions, thinly sliced
- 1 large carrot, julienne cut
- ½ cup broccoli, diced
- 3 red radishes, cut thin slices
- 1 garlic clove, minced
- 1 tsp each of dried oregano, salt, and black pepper
- 2 tbsp extra-virgin olive oil
- 2 chopped walnuts

Steps to Cook

1. Rinse the lettuce and coarsely chop it. Take a large bowl. Place all the ingredients on it—lettuce, cherry tomatoes, red onions, carrot, broccoli, red radish, and black olives.

2. To make salad dressing, take a small bowl, add extra virgin olive oil, and minced garlic clove. Mix well with a spoon.

3. Pour the dressing onto the chopped veggies and season with some dried oregano, salt, and black pepper. Toss well all the ingredients until combined.

4. Add chopped walnut and serve fresh.

Chapter 11: Salad Recipes

11.2 Citrus Kale Salad

TIME TO PREPARE
10 minutes

COOK TIME
0 minutes

SERVING
4 people

Nutritional Facts
134 kcal
20 gr Prot.

Ingredients

- 2 cups chopped fresh kale
- 1 cup pomegranate
- 2 small oranges, peeled and segmented
- 1 tbsp lemon juice, squeezed
- 1 tsp olive oil
- 1 garlic clove, minced
- ⅛ tsp salt
- ⅛ tsp black pepper

Steps to Cook

1. Wash the kale, remove the stem, and roughly chop the kale. In a large bowl, add the kale and olive oil and massage with clean hands. Massage as much as it is soft but still crispy.

2. Add segmented oranges and pomegranate to the kale to add some fun to the salad.

3. Take a small bowl and add lemon juice, salt, minced garlic, and black pepper. Mix well and pour into the mixture of kale, orange, and pomegranate.

4. Toss well all the ingredients and serve fresh.

Chapter 11: Salad Recipes

11.3 Body Reset Avocado Salad

TIME TO PREPARE

10 minutes

COOK TIME

0 minutes

SERVING

4 people

Nutritional Facts

133 kcal

20 gr Prot.

Ingredients

- 1 cup sliced avocados
- 1 cup cherry tomatoes
- ½ cup spinach leaves
- Salt to taste
- 1 tsp black pepper
- ¼ cup lemon juice

Steps to Cook

1. First, take a deep bowl and add sliced avocados, cherry tomatoes, and spinach leaves and mix them properly.
2. After that add salt to taste, black pepper, and lemon juice and mix it well and serve the avocado salad on the table.

Chapter 11: Salad Recipes

11.4 Tofu Berry Salad

TIME TO PREPARE

10 minutes

COOK TIME

0 minutes

SERVING

4 people

Nutritional Facts

112 kcal

22 gr Prot.

Ingredients

- 1 cup tofu
- ⅓ cup baby corn
- 1 tbsp sesame seeds
- ½ cup baby spinach leaves
- ½ cup lettuce leaves, shredded
- Chopped chives to taste
- 1 tbsp of olive oil
- Pepper to taste
- ⅓ cup cherry tomatoes
- 1 tsp mustard

Steps to Cook

1. Heat a grill pan over medium heat. Add sliced tofu and cook for approx. 10 minutes. Set aside and let cool.
2. Mix all ingredients (except mustard) in a large serving bowl. Also, add oil.
3. Combine mustard, top with cherry tomatoes, sprinkle some sesame seeds, and serve it.

Chapter 11: Salad Recipes

11.5 Brown Lentil Salad

TIME TO PREPARE

10 minutes

COOK TIME

0 minutes

SERVING

4 people

Nutritional Facts

137 kcal

25 gr Prot.

Ingredients

- 2 cups boiled brown lentils
- ½ cup tomato chopped
- 1 tsp coriander
- ½ cup carrot chopped
- 1 tsp green chili
- Salt to taste
- 1 tsp black pepper
- 1 tsp cumin seeds
- ½ cup lemon juice
- ¼ cup broccoli
- ¼ cup celery
- Onion

Steps to Cook

1. First, take a deep bowl and add boiled brown lentils.

2. Then add chopped tomato, onion, celery, broccoli, carrot, coriander, and green chili to the above mixture.

3. After that add salt to taste, black pepper, cumin seeds, and lemon juice and mix it well and serve brown lentil salad on the table.

4. Serve brown lentil salad fresh. Enjoy!

Chapter 11: Salad Recipes

11.6 Berry Salad

TIME TO PREPARE

10 minutes

COOK TIME

0 minutes

SERVING

4 people

Nutritional Facts

134 kcal

20 gr Prot.

Ingredients

- 1 cup strawberries
- 1 cup blueberries
- 1 cup walnuts
- 1 cup spinach leaves
- 1 tsp lemon juice
- 1 tsp honey

Steps to Cook

1. Take the berries and wash them properly. Then cut strawberries into half pieces. Take a large bowl and add strawberries, blueberries, spinach leaves, and walnuts in it and mix it properly.

2. Then add lemon juice and honey to the above salad and toss it again properly.

3. Take this berries salad out on the platter and serve it for the whole body reset diet.

11.7 Falafel Salad Bowl

TIME TO PREPARE

10 minutes

COOK TIME

0 minutes

SERVING

4 people

Nutritional Facts

112 kcal
22 gr Prot.

Ingredients

- 100 g boiled chickpea
- 50 g broad beans
- 50 g sliced tomatoes
- 50 g sliced carrots
- 50 g boiled corns
- 50 g hummus
- 100 g lettuce
- 1 tsp olive oil
- 1 tbsp lemon juice
- ¼ tsp salt
- Black pepper to taste

Steps to Cook

1. Take a small bowl and add olive oil, salt, and lemon juice and mix it properly and put aside.

2. Then take a food processor and add boiled chickpea, broad beans, salt, black pepper, and olive oil. Mix it and form balls. Then deep fry the falafel bowl and put it aside

3. Then take another bowl and add lettuce at the bottom of the bowl and then top it with falafel bowls, sliced tomatoes, carrots, boiled corn, and hummus side by side to fill the bowl.

4. Pour dressing over the falafel bowl. Serve it. Enjoy!

Chapter 11: Salad Recipes

11.8 Burrito Salad

TIME TO PREPARE

10 minutes

COOK TIME

0 minutes

SERVING

4 people

Nutritional Facts

167 kcal

20 gr Prot.

Ingredients

- 1 grilled chicken breast piece
- 50 g sliced avocado
- 50g sliced tomatoes
- 50g sliced capsicum
- 50 g boiled corns
- 50 g boiled kidney beans
- 50 g shredded cheese
- 50g Thousand Island sauce
- 100 g lettuce

Steps to Cook

1. Take a bowl and add lettuce at the bottom of the bowl and then top it with grilled chicken breast, sliced avocados, sliced tomatoes, capsicum, boiled corn, and kidney beans, side by side to fill the bowl.
2. Then sprinkle cheese over it.
3. Pour the Thousand Island sauce on it. Serve it.

Chapter 11: Salad Recipes

11.9 Body Reset Egg Salad

**TIME TO
PREPARE**

10 minutes

**COOK
TIME**

0 minutes

SERVING

4 people

**Nutritional
Facts**

145 kcal

25 gr Prot.

Ingredients

- 1 tsp olive oil
- 1 tbsp lemon juice
- 1 tsp salt
- 50 g sliced cucumbers
- 50 g sliced tomatoes
- 50 g sliced cabbage
- 50 g sliced onion
- 100 g spinach leaves
- 50 g sliced avocado
- 2 boiled eggs
- 1 tsp black pepper

Steps to Cook

1. Take a small bowl and add olive oil, salt, lemon juice and mix it properly and put it aside.
2. Take a bowl and add diced cucumbers, tomatoes, cabbage, onion, spinach leaves, and avocados side by side to fill the bowl.
3. Place boiled eggs in the above-prepared bowl.
4. Pour the above-prepared dressing on it. Serve it.

Chapter 11: Salad Recipes

11.10 Quinoa Vegetable Salad

TIME TO PREPARE

10 minutes

COOK TIME

0 minutes

SERVING

4 people

Nutritional Facts

113 kcal

20 gr Prot.

Ingredients

- 1 tsp olive oil
- 1 tbsp lemon juice
- 1 tsp salt
- 50 g diced cucumbers
- 50 g diced tomatoes
- 50 g sliced red cabbage
- 50 g sliced onion
- 50 g sweet potato cubes
- 200 g boiled quinoa

Steps to Cook

1. Take a small bowl and add olive oil, salt, and lemon juice, mix it properly, and put it aside.
2. Take a bowl and add diced cucumbers, tomatoes, cabbage, onion, boiled sweet potatoes cubes, and boiled quinoa side by side to fill the bowl.
3. Pour the above-prepared dressing on it. Serve it.

Chapter 11: Salad Recipes

11.11 Chicken Salad Bowl

TIME TO PREPARE

10 minutes

COOK TIME

0 minutes

SERVING

4 people

Nutritional Facts

156 kcal

27 gr Prot.

Ingredients

- 1 boneless skinless chicken breast
- 100 g romaine lettuce
- 50 g zucchini diced
- 50 g yellow squash
- 50 g red bell pepper
- 2 tsp taco seasoning
- 1 tsp olive oil
- 1 tsp chili powder
- 1 tsp cumin
- 1 tsp salt
- 50 g avocado sliced
- 2 tbsp salad dressing
- 4 tbsp salsa

Steps to Cook

1. Take chicken breast and season it with taco seasoning. Grill chicken for 10–12 minutes in the baking oven. Let rest for 5 minutes and then cut into slices.
2. Take a pan and add oil in it, heat it. Add peppers and cook 2–3 minutes. Then add zucchini and yellow squash. Then add cumin, chili powder, and salt and cook for 2–3 minutes.
3. Add lettuce to the bottom of each bowl. Add vegetables and chicken on top. Add dressing or salsa. Serve chicken salad bowl. Enjoy!

Chapter 11: Salad Recipes

11.12 Shrimp Salad

TIME TO PREPARE

10 minutes

COOK TIME

0 minutes

SERVING

4 people

Nutritional Facts

134 kcal

27 gr Prot.

Ingredients

- 100 g grilled shrimps
- 50 g sliced avocado
- 50 g sliced tomatoes
- 50 g sliced capsicum
- 50 g chopped cabbage
- 50 g chopped onion
- 100 g lettuce
- 1 tsp olive oil
- 1 tbsp lemon juice
- ¼ tsp salt

Steps to Cook

1. Take a small bowl and add olive oil, salt, and lemon juice, mix it properly, and put aside.

2. Take a bowl and add lettuce at the bottom of the bowl and then top it with grilled shrimps, chopped cabbage, chopped onion, sliced avocados, sliced tomatoes, and capsicum side by side to fill the bowl.

3. Pour the dressing over the bowl. Serve it. Enjoy!

Chapter 11: Salad Recipes

11.13 Sweet Potato Salad

TIME TO PREPARE

10 minutes

COOK TIME

0 minutes

SERVING

4 people

Nutritional Facts

117 kcal

20 gr Prot.

Ingredients

- 100 g boiled sweet potato cubes
- 50 g sliced green onion
- 50 g sliced capsicum
- 200 g boiled brown rice
- 100 g lettuce
- Sesame seeds for garnish

Steps to Cook

1. Take a bowl and add boiled rice at the bottom of the bowl and then top it with boiled sweet potato cubes, lettuce leaves, green onions, and sliced capsicum side by side to fill the bowl. Mix it all.
2. Garnish sweet potato salad with sesame seeds. Serve it. Enjoy!

Chapter 11: Salad Recipes

11.14 Salmon Salad

TIME TO PREPARE

10 minutes

COOK TIME

0 minutes

SERVING

4 people

Nutritional Facts

145 kcal

27 gr Prot.

Ingredients

- 100 g grilled salmon
- 50 g avocado cubes
- 50 g sliced tomatoes
- 50 g sliced capsicum
- 50 g boiled green beans
- 1 tsp olive oil
- 1 tbsp lemon juice
- ¼ tsp salt
- Sesame seeds for garnish

Steps to Cook

1. Take a small bowl and add olive oil, salt, lemon juice, and mix it very well and put aside.

2. Take a bowl and add grilled salmon, avocados, sliced tomatoes, capsicum, and boiled green beans side by side to fill the bowl.

3. Pour dressing over the bowl. Garnish the salmon salad with sesame seeds. Serve it. Enjoy!

Chapter 11: Salad Recipes

11.15 Chicken and Bulgur Salad Bowl

TIME TO PREPARE

10 minutes

COOK TIME

0 minutes

SERVING

4 people

Nutritional Facts

157 kcal

28 gr Prot.

Ingredients

- 100 g bulgur
- 50 g sliced avocado
- 50 g sliced tomatoes
- 50 g sliced capsicum
- 50 g cucumber cubes
- 100 g chicken cubes
- 1 tsp olive oil
- 1 tbsp lemon juice
- ¼ tsp salt
- 1 tbsp black pepper
- Lettuce

Steps to Cook

1. Take a bowl and add chicken cubes. Marinate it with salt, black pepper, and lemon juice and put aside for 1 hour. Grease a pan with oil and cook the chicken. Cut into slices. Then take a small bowl and add olive oil, salt, lemon juice, and black pepper, mix it properly, and put it aside.

2. Then take a saucepan, boil water and bulgur and cook for 10 minutes. Then strain the water. Then take a bowl and add lettuce at the bottom of the bowl and then top it with bulgur, grilled chicken, sliced avocados, sliced tomatoes, capsicum, and cucumber cubes side by side to fill the bowl.

3. Pour dressing over the chicken and bulgur salad bowl. Serve it. Enjoy!

Chapter 11: Salad Recipes

11.16 Grilled Chicken Salsa Bowl

TIME TO PREPARE
10 minutes

COOK TIME
0 minutes

SERVING
4 people

Nutritional Facts
147 kcal
28 gr Prot.

Ingredients

- 1 cup butternut squash
- 50 g boiled red beans
- 50 g chopped tomatoes
- 50 g boiled corns
- 50 g lettuce
- 1 tsp olive oil
- 1 tbsp lemon juice
- ¼ tsp salt
- ½ tsp chili flakes
- Coriander for garnish
- 1 chicken breast
- 1 tsp black pepper

Steps to Cook

1. Take a bowl and add chicken breast. Marinate it with salt, black pepper, and lemon juice and put aside for 1 hour. Grease a pan with oil and cook the chicken. Cut it into slices. Then take a small bowl and add olive oil, salt, lemon juice, and chili flakes, mix it properly, and put it aside.

2. Take a bowl and add butternut squash cubes, chicken pieces, tomatoes, lettuce, red beans, and corn side by side to fill the bowl. Mix it properly.

3. Pour the above-prepared dressing over the grilled chicken salsa bowl. Garnish with coriander. Serve it. Enjoy!

Chapter 11: Salad Recipes

11.17 Chipotle Chicken Salad

TIME TO PREPARE

10 minutes

COOK TIME

0 minutes

SERVING

4 people

Nutritional Facts

157 kcal

28 gr Prot.

Ingredients

- 50 g avocadoes
- 50 g boiled red beans
- 50 g cherry tomatoes
- 50 g boiled corns
- 50 g lettuce
- 1 tsp olive oil
- 1 tbsp lemon juice
- ¼ tsp salt
- 1 chicken breast
- 1 tsp black pepper
- 1 tbsp chipotle sauce

Steps to Cook

1. Take a bowl and add chicken breast. Marinate it with salt, black pepper, and lemon juice and put aside for 1 hour. Grease a pan with oil and cook the chicken. Cut it into slices.

2. Take a bowl and add chicken pieces, cherry tomatoes, lettuce, red beans, avocadoes, and corn side by side to fill the bowl.

3. Pour chipotle sauce over the chipotle chicken salad bowl. Serve it. Enjoy!

11.18 Mexican Chicken Salad

TIME TO PREPARE

10 minutes

COOK TIME

0 minutes

SERVING

4 people

Nutritional Facts

145 kcal

30 gr Prot.

Ingredients

- ½ cup boiled corns
- 50 g cherry tomatoes
- 50 g lettuce
- 1 tsp olive oil
- 1 tbsp lemon juice
- ¼ tsp salt
- ½ tsp Mexican seasoning
- Sesame seeds for garnish
- 1 chicken breast
- 1 tsp black pepper
- Chili flakes

Steps to Cook

1. Take a bowl and add chicken breast. Marinate it with the Mexican seasoning, salt, black pepper, and lemon juice and put it aside for 1 hour. Grease a pan with oil and cook the chicken. Cut into slices.

2. Then take a small bowl and add olive oil, salt, lemon juice, chili flakes and mix it properly and put it aside.

3. Take a bowl and add boiled corns, chicken pieces, tomatoes, and lettuce side by side to fill the bowl.

4. Pour the above-prepared dressing over the Mexican chicken Salad and garnish with sesame seeds. Serve it. Enjoy!

Chapter 11: Salad Recipes

11.19 Chicken Fajita Salad

**TIME TO
PREPARE**

10 minutes

**COOK
TIME**

10 minutes

SERVING

4 people

**Nutritional
Facts**

145 kcal

30 gr Prot.

Ingredients

- 200 g grilled chicken
- 50 g cherry tomatoes
- 50 g sliced green capsicum
- 50 g sliced yellow capsicum
- 50 g sliced red capsicum
- 1 tsp olive oil
- 1 tbsp lemon juice
- ¼ tsp salt
- 1 tbsp fajita sauce
- 1 cup lettuce

Steps to Cook

1. Take a small bowl and add fajita sauce, olive oil, salt, and lemon juice and mix it properly and put it aside.

2. Take a bowl and add lettuce at the bottom of the bowl and then top it with grilled chicken, cherry tomatoes, and sliced green, yellow and red capsicum side by side to fill the bowl. Mix it properly.

3. Pour dressing over the chicken fajita salad and mix it properly. Serve it. Enjoy!

Chapter 11: Salad Recipes

11.20 Chicken Caesar Salad

TIME TO PREPARE

10 minutes

COOK TIME

0 minutes

SERVING

4 people

Nutritional Facts

133 kcal

25 gr Prot.

Ingredients

- 200g grilled chicken
- 50g cherry tomatoes
- 50 g sliced green capsicum
- 50 g sliced yellow capsicum
- 50 g sliced red capsicum
- 1 tsp olive oil
- 1 tbsp lemon juice
- ¼ tsp salt
- 1 tbsp Thousand Island sauce
- 1 cup lettuce leaves

Steps to Cook

1. Take a small bowl and add Thousand Island sauce, olive oil, salt, lemon juice and mix it properly and put it aside.

2. Take a bowl and add lettuce at the bottom of the bowl and then top it with grilled chicken, cherry tomatoes, and sliced green, yellow and red capsicum side by side to fill the bowl. Mix it properly.

3. Pour dressing over the chicken Caesar salad and mix it properly. Serve it. Enjoy!

Chapter 11: Salad Recipes

11.21 Poke Salad Bowl

TIME TO PREPARE
10 minutes

COOK TIME
0 minutes

SERVING
4 people

Nutritional Facts
113 kcal
25 gr Prot.

Ingredients

- 100 g boiled rice
- 100 g salmon cubes
- 50 g avocado cubes
- 1 tsp olive oil
- 1 tbsp lemon juice
- ¼ tsp salt

Steps to Cook

1. Take a small bowl and add olive oil, salt, and lemon juice and mix it properly and put it aside.

2. Take a bowl and add boiled rice at the bottom of the bowl and then top it with salmon cubes and avocados cubes, side by side to fill the bowl.

3. Pour dressing over the easy poke salad bowl. Serve it. Enjoy!

Chapter 11: Salad Recipes

11.22 Tuna Salad

TIME TO PREPARE

10 minutes

COOK TIME

0 minutes

SERVING

4 people

Nutritional Facts

154 kcal

25 gr Prot.

Ingredients

- 100 g boiled rice
- 100 g tuna fish cubes
- 50 g avocado cubes
- 1 tsp olive oil
- 1 tbsp lemon juice
- ¼ tsp salt
- ½ tsp paprika
- Sesame seeds to garnish
- Coriander leaves to garnish

Steps to Cook

1. Take a small bowl and add paprika, olive oil, salt, and lemon juice, mix it properly, and put it aside.

2. Take a bowl and add boiled rice at the bottom of the bowl and then top it with tuna fish cubes and avocado cubes. Garnish it with sesame seeds and coriander leaves. Mix it properly.

3. Pour dressing over the tuna salad.

4. Serve it. Enjoy!

Chapter 11: Salad Recipes

11.23 Shrimp Pasta Salad

TIME TO PREPARE

10 minutes

COOK TIME

0 minutes

SERVING

4 people

Nutritional Facts

178 kcal

25 gr Prot.

Ingredients

- 1 lb grilled shrimps
- 1 cup boiled pasta
- ½ cup chopped tomato
- 1 tsp coriander
- ⅓ cup carrot chopped
- 1 tsp green chili
- Salt to taste
- 1 tsp black pepper
- 1 tsp cumin seeds
- ½ cup lemon juice
- ¼ cup broccoli
- ¼ cup celery
- Onion

Steps to Cook

1. First, take the deep bowl and add boiled pasta and the grilled shrimp.
2. Then add chopped tomato, onion, celery, broccoli, carrot, coriander, and green chili to the above mixture.
3. After that add salt to taste, black pepper, cumin seeds, and lemon juice and mix it well and serve brown lentil salad on the table.
4. Serve brown lentil salad fresh. Enjoy!

Chapter 11: Salad Recipes

11.24 Chickpea Salad

TIME TO PREPARE

10 minutes

COOK TIME

0 minutes

SERVING

4 people

Nutritional Facts

153 kcal

25 gr Prot.

Ingredients

- 2 cups boiled chickpea
- ½ cup chopped tomato
- 1 tsp coriander
- ½ cup chopped onion
- 1 tsp green chili
- Salt to taste
- 1 tsp black pepper
- 1 tsp cumin seeds
- ⅓ cup lemon juice
- Potato boiled
- ½ cup cucumber

Steps to Cook

1. First, take the deep bowl and add boiled chickpea.
2. Then add potato cubes, chopped tomato, onion, coriander, cucumber, and green chili to the boiled chickpeas.
3. After that add salt to taste, black pepper, cumin seeds, and lemon juice and mix it well and serve it on the table.
4. Enjoy!

Chapter 11: Salad Recipes

11.25 Avocado Kale Salad

TIME TO PREPARE

10 minutes

COOK TIME

0 minutes

SERVING

4 people

Nutritional Facts

117 kcal

20 gr Prot.

Ingredients

- 2 large cucumbers, sliced
- 2 large avocados,peeled, pitted, and sliced
- ¾ cup chives
- 1 cup kale
- 2 garlic cloves, minced
- 2 tbsp lemon juice
- 2 tbsp olive oil
- 1 tsp sea salt
- 1 tsp black pepper
- Fresh parsley

Steps to Cook

3. In a large bowl combine cucumber, kale, sliced avocado, and chives.
4. In a small bowl, add lemon juice, salt, minced garlic, and black pepper. Mix well.
5. Pour the dressing over cucumber and avocado and toss well.
6. Drizzle with some olive oil and mix with a wooden spoon.
7. In a serving bowl spread fresh parsley, and transfer the salad to it.
8. Serve immediately.

Chapter 11: Salad Recipes

11.26 Papaya Kale Salad

TIME TO PREPARE

10 minutes

COOK TIME

0 minutes

SERVING

4 people

Nutritional Facts

117 kcal

20 gr Prot.

Ingredients

- 1 bunch kale, cut into thin ribbons
- 1 tbsp lemon juice, squeezed
- 1 tbsp extra-virgin olive oil
- ½ tsp pink salt
- ¼ cup grated fresh vegan cheese
- 1 small onion, thin slices
- ¼ cup papaya cubes
- ¼ cup brown rice

Steps to Cook

1. Wash the kale, remove the stem, and slice the kale into thin ribbons.
2. In a large bowl combine the kale and olive oil and massage with clean hands. Massage as much as it is soft but still crispy.
3. Add papaya, onion, brown rice, and parmesan cheese.
4. Toss well all the ingredients with lemon juice and salt and serve fresh.

Chapter 11: Salad Recipes

11.27 Grilled Butternut Squash Salad

TIME TO PREPARE
10 minutes

COOK TIME
0 minutes

SERVING
4 people

Nutritional Facts
134 kcal
20 gr Prot.

Ingredients

- 1 butternut squash, peeled and seeded
- 2 tbsp coconut oil
- 2 garlic cloves, minced
- ¼ tsp salt
- ⅛ tsp black pepper
- 1 tbsp parsley, finely chopped
- ½ cup boiled chickpeas
- 1 beetroot
- Cheese

Steps to Cook

1. Preheat the oven to 375°F.

2. Cut the butternut squash into cubes.

3. Take a large bowl and combine butternut squash with coconut oil and garlic cloves.

4. Season with salt and black pepper and toss well.

5. Place the seasoned butternut squash on a baking sheet and roast in the oven for about 20–30 minutes until it gets soft and light brown.

6. Take a large bowl and add boiled chickpea, salt, black pepper, squash, cheese, and beetroot and mix it properly.

7. Place it on the serving plate, garnish with parsley, and serve.

Chapter 11: Salad Recipes

11.28 Stuffed-Avocado Salad

TIME TO PREPARE
10 minutes

COOK TIME
0 minutes

SERVING
4 people

Nutritional Facts
117 kcal
20 gr Prot.

Ingredients

- 2 avocados, halved
- ½ cup cherry tomatoes, cut into **slices**
- ½ cup small yellow tomatoes, cut into slices
- 1 tbsp olive oil
- 1 tsp salt
- 1 tsp grounded black pepper
- 1 tsp oregano
- 1 tsp thyme
- 1 tsp garlic powder
- 5–6 fresh basil leaves

Steps to Cook

1. Take a large mixing bowl and add tomatoes, salt, black pepper, oregano, thyme, garlic powder, and olive oil. Mix properly with the fork.
2. Lay down the avocado halves on a plate. Scoop out some avocado flesh to make a hole.
3. Transfer the mixture to avocados. Garnish with basil leaves and serve.

Chapter 11: Salad Recipes

11.29 Red Beans and Chickpea Salad

TIME TO PREPARE

10 minutes

COOK TIME

0 minutes

SERVING

4 people

Nutritional Facts

167 kcal

23 gr Prot.

Ingredients

- 1 cup boiled red beans
- ½ cup boiled corn
- 1–2 red chilies
- ½ cup boiled chickpea
- 1 tsp olive oil
- Salt to taste
- 1 tsp black pepper
- 1 tsp chopped coriander
- 1 tsp cumin seeds
- ½ cup lemon juice
- 1 boiled potato

Steps to Cook

1. First, take a deep bowl and add boiled chickpea, corns, red beans, red chilies, and boiled potato cubes in it.
2. Then add coriander to the above bowl and mix it very well.
3. After that add salt to taste, black pepper, cumin seeds, olive oil, and lemon juice, mix it well, and serve red beans and chickpea salad on the table.
4. Serve it. Enjoy!

Chapter 11: Salad Recipes

11.30 Body Reset Corn Salad

TIME TO PREPARE
10 minutes

COOK TIME
0 minutes

SERVING
4 people

Nutritional Facts
134 kcal
23 gr Prot.

Ingredients

- 2 cups boiled quinoa
- ½ cup tomato chopped
- 1 tsp coriander
- ½ cup onion chopped
- 1 tsp green chili
- Salt to taste
- 1 tsp black pepper
- 1 tsp cumin seeds
- ½ cup lemon juice
- 2 boiled potatoes
- ½ cup cucumber
- 1 cup boiled corn

Steps to Cook

1. First, take a deep bowl and add boiled quinoa.

2. Then add boiled corn, potato cubes, chopped tomato, onion, coriander, green chili, and chopped cucumber to the boiled quinoa.

3. After that add salt to taste, black pepper, cumin seeds, and lemon Juice, mix it well, and serve the body reset corn salad on the table.

4. Enjoy!

Chapter 11: Salad Recipes

11.31 Julienne-Cut Salad

TIME TO PREPARE
10 minutes

COOK TIME
0 minutes

SERVING
4 people

Nutritional Facts
117 kcal
20 gr Prot.

Ingredients	Steps to Cook
<ul><li>1 cup sliced red cabbage</li><li>½ cup sliced carrot</li><li>1 tsp coriander</li><li>½ cup sliced cucumber</li><li>1 tsp sliced green chili</li><li>Salt to taste</li><li>1 tsp black pepper</li><li>1 tsp cumin seeds</li><li>½ cup lemon juice</li></ul>	1. First, take a deep bowl and add sliced red cabbage, sliced carrot, and sliced cucumber. 2. Then add coriander and green chili to the above mixture. 3. Then, add salt to taste, black pepper, cumin seeds, and lemon juice and mix it well and serve the salad on the table. 4. Enjoy!

Chapter 11: Salad Recipes

11.32 Cherry Tomato and Cucumber Herb Salad

**TIME TO
PREPARE**

10 minutes

**COOK
TIME**

0 minutes

SERVING

4 people

**Nutritional
Facts**

144 kcal

22 gr Prot.

Ingredients

- 2 cups cucumber
- 1 cup cherry tomatoes
- 1 tbsp coriander
- 1 tsp green chili
- Salt to taste
- 1 tsp black pepper
- 1 tsp cumin seeds
- ½ cup lemon juice
- 1 tbsp celery
- 1 tbsp parsley
- 2 tbsp mixed fresh herbs (any)

Steps to Cook

1. First, take the deep bowl and add chopped cucumber.
2. Then add cherry tomatoes, coriander, green chili, celery, parsley, and mix fresh herbs and mix it properly.
3. Then, add salt to taste, black pepper, cumin seeds, and lemon Juice, mix it well, and serve cucumber salad with fresh herbs on the table.
4. Enjoy!

Chapter 11: Salad Recipes

11.33 Mango Kale Salad

TIME TO PREPARE

10 minutes

COOK TIME

0 minutes

SERVING

4 people

Nutritional Facts

127 kcal

20 gr Prot.

Ingredients

- 1 cup mango chopped
- ½ cup red cabbage
- 1 cup kale
- 1 cup lettuce leaves
- ½ cup iceberg cubes
- Salt to taste
- 1 tsp black pepper
- 1 tsp cumin seeds
- ½ cup lemon juice

Steps to Cook

1. First, take a deep bowl and add chopped mangoes.

2. Then add red cabbage, kale, lettuce leaves, and iceberg cubes and mix it properly.

3. Then, add salt to taste, black pepper, cumin seeds, and lemon juice, mix it well, and serve fresh mango salad on the table.

4. Enjoy!

Chapter 11: Salad Recipes

11.34 Red Cabbage and Carrot Salad

TIME TO PREPARE

10 minutes

COOK TIME

0 minutes

SERVING

4 people

Nutritional Facts

67 kcal

15 gr Prot.

Ingredients

- 2 cups sliced red cabbage
- ½ cup sliced carrot
- 1 tsp coriander
- ½ cup sliced onion
- ½ cup sliced beetroot
- 1 tsp sliced green chili
- Salt to taste
- 1 tsp black pepper
- 1 tsp sesame seeds
- ½ cup lemon juice
- 1 tbsp extra-virgin olive oil

Steps to Cook

1. First, take a deep bowl and add sliced red cabbage, sliced carrot, coriander, sliced onions, and sliced beetroot.
2. Then add green chili to the above mixture.
3. After that add salt to taste, black pepper, sesame seeds, extra virgin olive oil, and lemon juice, mix it well, and serve the red cabbage and carrot salad on the table.
4. Enjoy!

Chapter 11: Salad Recipes

11.35 Citrus Beetroot Salad

TIME TO PREPARE

10 minutes

COOK TIME

0 minutes

SERVING

4 people

Nutritional Facts

134 kcal

20 gr Prot.

Ingredients

- 1 cup peeled orange slices
- 1 cup grapefruit slices
- ½ cup spinach chopped
- 1 tsp coriander
- ½ cup chopped lettuce leaves
- ¼ cup boiled beans
- Salt to taste
- 1 tsp black pepper
- 1 tsp cumin seeds
- ½ cup lemon juice
- ¼ cup vegan cheese/tofu
- ¼ cup chopped beetroot

Steps to Cook

1. First, take a deep bowl and add peeled orange, spinach, lettuce leaves, and boiled beans and mix it properly.
2. Then add coriander, chopped beetroot, grapefruit, and vegan cheese and mix it properly.
3. Then add salt to taste, black pepper, cumin seeds, and lemon Juice, mix it well, and serve the citrus salad on the table.
4. Enjoy!

Chapter 11: Salad Recipes

11.36 Pickled Sweet potato and Beetroot Salad

TIME TO PREPARE
10 minutes

COOK TIME
0 minutes

SERVING
4 people

Nutritional Facts
133 kcal
20 gr Prot.

Ingredients

- 1 cup beetroot cubes
- ½ cup tomato chopped
- 1 tsp coriander
- 1 tsp green chili
- Salt to taste
- 1 tsp black pepper
- 1 tsp cumin seeds
- ½ cup lemon juice
- 2 boiled potato cubes
- 1 cup pickled cucumber
- ¼ cup walnuts

Steps to Cook

1. First, take a deep bowl and add beetroot cubes, tomatoes, potato cubes, and pickled cucumber and mix it properly.

2. Then add coriander, green chili, and walnuts to the above mixture.

3. Then, add salt to taste, black pepper, cumin seeds, and lemon juice, mix it well, and serve the potato beetroot salad with pickled cucumber on the table.

Chapter 11: Salad Recipes

11.37 Spinach Apple Walnut Salad

TIME TO PREPARE

10 minutes

COOK TIME

0 minutes

SERVING

4 people

Nutritional Facts

133 kcal

20 gr Prot

Ingredients

- 2 apples
- ½ cup spinach leaves
- ¼ cup walnuts
- ½ cup chopped cabbage
- 1 tsp lemon juice
- 1 tsp black pepper
- 1 cup pomegranate

Steps to Cook

1. Take the apples and cut them into slices.

2. Wash the spinach leaves properly with water.

3. Now, take a large bowl and add apple slices, spinach leaves, walnuts, cabbage, and pomegranate and mix it properly.

4. Season apple salad with lemon juice and black pepper. Garnish it with walnuts and serve it.

5. Enjoy!

Chapter 11: Salad Recipes

11.38 Broccoli Salad

TIME TO PREPARE

10 minutes

COOK TIME

0 minutes

SERVING

4 people

Nutritional Facts

123 kcal

20 gr Prot

Ingredients

- 1 cup broccoli
- 1 tsp orange zest
- ¼ cup onion slices
- ½ cup boiled chickpeas
- ¼ cup iceberg
- 1 tsp olive oil
- 1 tsp lemon juice
- Salt to taste
- 1 tsp black pepper

Steps to Cook

1. Take broccoli in a bowl and wash it properly under tap water.
2. Now cut the broccoli in half.
3. Take a bowl and add broccoli, onion slices, boiled chickpeas, and iceberg cubes in it and mix it properly.
4. Now add orange zest, olive oil, lemon juice, salt, and black pepper and mix it again.
5. Garnish the broccoli salad with orange zest and serve it immediately.
6. Enjoy!

Chapter 11: Salad Recipes

11.39 Rainbow Peanut Salad

TIME TO PREPARE
10 minutes

COOK TIME
0 minutes

SERVING
4 people

Nutritional Facts
122 kcal
20 gr Prot

Ingredients

- 1 tsp lemon juice
- 1 tsp olive oil
- ½ cup peanuts
- ¼ cup onion slices
- ¼ cup tomato slices
- ¼ cup cabbage slices
- 2 tbsp coriander
- ¼ cup yellow capsicum
- ½ cup iceberg

Steps to Cook

1. Take a large bowl and add all vegetables, onion slices, tomato slices, cabbage slices, coriander, yellow capsicum, and iceberg and mix it properly.

2. Now add roasted peanuts to this bowl and mix it again.

3. Now season Thai salad with lemon juice and olive oil. Garnish it with roasted peanuts. Serve it immediately.

4. Enjoy!

Chapter 11: Salad Recipes

11.40 Ultimate Fruit Salad

TIME TO PREPARE
10 minutes

COOK TIME
0 minutes

SERVING
4 people

Nutritional Facts
135 kcal
25 gr Prot

Ingredients

- 1 papaya, cut into small pieces
- 1 pineapple, cut into small pieces
- 1-quart fresh strawberries, washed, hulled, halved
- 1-quart fresh raspberries, washed, hulled, halved
- 3 cups berries, your favorite kind
- Any other fruit you enjoy or that is in season

Steps to Cook

1. First cut fruits into small pieces. Store then each type of fruit separately, in different Ziplock bags.

2. Take a large bowl and mix all fruits in it. Refrigerate the bowl with the fruit until ready to serve.

3. When ready to serve, serve it immediately for salad.

4. Enjoy!

Chapter 12:
Sandwiches for Whole Body Reset Diet

Chapter 12: Sandwich Recipes

12.1 Grilled Tofu Sandwich

TIME TO PREPARE

10 minutes

COOK TIME

10 minutes

SERVING

4 people

Nutritional Facts

147 kcal

30 gr Prot.

Ingredients

- 1 pack of tofu, cut into bite size
- 1 sliced tomato
- 1 onion, thin slices
- 2–3 lettuce leaves
- 1 tsp salt
- 1 tsp coconut oil
- 1 tsp black pepper
- 2 bran bread slices
- 1 tbsp vegan mayonnaise
- 1 tbsp hummus

Steps to Cook

1. Take a pan, heat the oil, and cook both sides of tofu for about 2–3 minutes until light brown. Sprinkle some salt and black pepper on both sides.
2. On the same pan toast the bread.
3. In a bowl mix vegan mayonnaise and hummus.
4. Spread mayonnaise and hummus mixture on both toasts.
5. Firstly, place lettuce, tofu, tomatoes, and onion slices.
6. Place the other toast on the assembled toast. Serve immediately and enjoy.

Chapter 12: Sandwich Recipes

12.2 Peanut Butter Sandwich

TIME TO PREPARE

10 minutes

COOK TIME

10 minutes

SERVING

4 people

Nutritional Facts

166 kcal

30 gr Prot.

Ingredients

- 4 bran bread slices
- 2 banana
- 4 tbsp peanut butter
- 1 tsp vegetable oil

Steps to Cook

1. First, take a pan and grease it with vegetable oil. Now place it on medium heat.

2. Now add bread slices to the pan and toss them from both sides until it turns light golden.

3. Now remove it from heat and spread peanut butter over all the slices of bread.

4. Cut banana into slices and spread it on one side and then place the other bread slice over it. Cut it in half and serve it immediately.

5. Enjoy!

Chapter 12: Sandwich Recipes

12.3 Body Reset Salad Sandwich

TIME TO PREPARE

10 minutes

COOK TIME

10 minutes

SERVING

4 people

Nutritional Facts

147 kcal

30 gr Prot.

Ingredients

- 2 bran bread slices
- 2–3 spinach leaves
- 4–6 tomato slices
- 4–5 avocado slices
- 2 tbsp celery
- ¼ cup chickpea
- ¼ cup red cabbage
- 1 cup boiled and mashed potato
- 2 tbsp mayonnaise

Steps to Cook

1. First, take a pan and put it on medium heat. Then place bread slices over the pan and toss bread slices from both sides.

2. Now spread mayonnaise on both slices of bread. Then add spinach slices, tomato slices, avocado slices, celery, boiled chickpea, red cabbage, and mashed potato layer by layer.

3. Then place the other bread slice over it, gently press, and then cut the vegan rainbow sandwich in half with the help of a knife. Serve it immediately. Enjoy!

Chapter 12: Sandwich Recipes

12.4 Grilled Chicken Sandwich

TIME TO PREPARE

10 minutes

COOK TIME

10 minutes

SERVING

4 people

Nutritional Facts

147 kcal

30 gr Prot.

Ingredients

- 2 bran bread slices
- 2–3 cabbage leaves
- 4–6 tomato slices
- Salt to taste
- 1 lb chicken breast
- 1 tsp black pepper
- 1 cup boiled and sliced potato
- 2 tbsp mayonnaise
- 1 tsp vegetable oil
- 2 tbsp olives

Steps to Cook

1. First, take a grilling pan and grease it with oil. Then place chicken breast, cabbage, tomato, and boiled potato slices over it and grill it on medium heat.

2. Now spread mayonnaise on both slices of bread. Then add grilled cabbage slices, tomato slices, olives, and sliced grilled potato layer by layer on 1 slice of bread. Then sprinkle salt and black pepper over it.

3. Then place the other bread slice over it and gently press it and grill it on the grilling pan until it shows marks, then cut the grilled sandwich in half with the help of a knife. Serve it immediately. Enjoy!

Chapter 12: Sandwich Recipes

12.5 Chickpea Sandwich

TIME TO PREPARE

10 minutes

COOK TIME

10 minutes

SERVING

4 people

Nutritional Facts

144 kcal

30 gr Prot.

Ingredients

- 2 bran bread slices
- 1 tsp lemon juice
- ¼ cup avocado mashed
- Salt to taste
- 1 tsp black pepper
- 2 tbsp celery
- ½ cup boiled chickpea
- 2 tbsp mayonnaise
- 1 tsp sesame seeds

Steps to Cook

1. First, take a pan and put it on medium heat. Then place bread slices over the pan and toss bread slices from both sides.

2. Now spread mayonnaise on both slices of bread. Then add mashed avocado and celery and sprinkle salt, black pepper, and lemon juice over it. Add boiled chickpea and sesame seeds.

3. Then place the other bread slice over it and gently press it and then cut the chickpea sandwich in half with the help of a knife. Serve it immediately. Enjoy!

Chapter 12: Sandwich Recipes

12.6 Mushroom Sandwich

TIME TO PREPARE

10 minutes

COOK TIME

10 minutes

SERVING

4 people

Nutritional Facts

157 kcal

30 gr Prot.

Ingredients

- 2 bran bread slices
- Salt to taste
- 1 tsp black pepper
- 1 tsp vinegar
- 1 tsp paprika powder
- 1 cup mushrooms
- 1 cup low-fat cheese
- 1 tsp vegetable oil

Steps to Cook

1. First, take a pan and put it on medium heat. Then place bread slices over the pan and toss bread slices from bothsides.

2. Now take a pan and put oil in it and place it on medium heat. Then add mushrooms and sauté for 5 minutes. Add salt, black pepper, vinegar, paprika, and low-fat cheese and mix it well. Place it on a bread slice. Then, place the other bread slice over it, gently press it, and then cut the vegan mushroom sandwich in half with the help of a knife.

3. Serve it immediately. Enjoy!

Chapter 12: Sandwich Recipes

12.7 Avocado Sandwich

TIME TO PREPARE

10 minutes

COOK TIME

10 minutes

SERVING

4 people

Nutritional Facts

144 kcal

25 gr Prot.

Ingredients

- 2 bran bread slices
- 1 tsp lemon juice
- ¼ cup avocado mashed
- Salt to taste
- 1 tsp black pepper
- ¼ cup cucumber slices
- 2 3 spinach leaves

Steps to Cook

1. First, take a pan and put it on medium heat. Then place bread slices over the pan and toss bread slices from both sides.

2. Now take a bowl and add mashed avocado and sprinkle salt, black pepper, and lemon juice over it. Spread it on bread slices and then add cucumber and spinach leaves.

3. Then place other bread slices over it and gently press it and then cut the avocado sandwich in half with the help of a knife.

4. Serve it immediately. Enjoy!

Chapter 12: Sandwich Recipes

12.8 Potato Patty Sandwich

TIME TO PREPARE
10 minutes

COOK TIME
10 minutes

SERVING
4 people

Nutritional Facts
146 kcal
30 gr Prot.

Ingredients

- 2 bran burger bun
- 2-3 spinach leaves
- 4-6 cucumber slices
- Salt to taste
- 1 tsp black pepper
- 1 tsp paprika
- 1 tsp oil
- 1 cup boiled and mashed potato
- 2 tbsp mayonnaise

Steps to Cook

1. First, take a pan and put it on medium heat. Then place the burger bun over the pan and toss the burger bun from both sides.
2. Take a bowl and add mashed potato, salt, black pepper, and paprika and mix it well. Make patties of it. Heat the oil in a pan and fry the potato patties from both sides.
3. Take burger bun and spread mayonnaise. Then place potato patty, spinach, and cucumber over it.
4. Serve it hot. Enjoy!

Chapter 12: Sandwich Recipes

12.9 Red Beans Ball Sandwich

TIME TO PREPARE

10 minutes

COOK TIME

10 minutes

SERVING

4 people

Nutritional Facts

145 kcal

30 gr Prot.

Ingredients

- 2 bran bread slices
- 2–3 spinach leaves
- 4–6 tomato slices
- Salt to taste
- 1 tsp black pepper
- 1 tsp paprika
- ¼ cup red cabbage
- 1 cup boiled and mashed red beans
- 2 tbsp mayonnaise

Steps to Cook

1. First, take a pan and put it on medium heat. Then place bread slices over the pan and toss bread slices from both sides.
2. Take a bowl and add mashed red beans, salt, black pepper, and paprika. Make small balls of it and fry it. Now spread mayonnaise on both slices of bread. Then add red beans balls, spinach slices, tomato slices, and red cabbage layer by layer.
3. Then place other bread slices over it and gently press it and then cut the red bean ball sandwich in half with the help of a knife.
4. Serve it immediately. Enjoy!

Chapter 12: Sandwich Recipes

12.10 Sloppy Joe Sandwich

TIME TO PREPARE
10 minutes

COOK TIME
10 minutes

SERVING
4 people

Nutritional Facts
155 kcal
30 gr Prot.

Ingredients

- 2 bran sandwich bread
- 2 tbsp mustard sauce
- 2 tbsp coriander leaves
- 1 tbsp mint sauce
- ¼ cup carrot sliced
- ¼ cup jalapeno
- 1 cup boiled green lentils
- Salt to taste
- 1 tsp black pepper
- 1 tsp vinegar
- 1 tsp paprika
- 1 tbsp oil

Steps to Cook

1. First, take a pan and put it on medium heat. Then place sandwich bread over the pan and toss it from both sides.

2. Now spread mustard and mint sauce on sandwich bread and put aside. Take a pan and heat some oil in it. Then add green lentils, salt, black pepper, paprika, and vinegar and cook it for 5 minutes.

3. Then, take the sandwich bread and put the previous mixture above it. Then add coriander, carrot, and jalapeno. Fold the sandwich.

4. Serve the Sloppy Joe Sandwich immediately. Enjoy it with mint sauce.

Chapter 12: Sandwich Recipes

12.11 Falafel Stuffed Sandwich

TIME TO PREPARE
10 minutes

COOK TIME
10 minutes

SERVING
4 people

Nutritional Facts
146 kcal
30 gr Prot.

Ingredients

- 2 bran sandwich bread
- ¼ cup cucumber slices
- 4–6 tomato slices
- 4–5 avocado slices
- 2 tbsp celery
- ¼ cup boiled chickpea
- ¼ cup red cabbage
- 1 tsp oil
- ½ cup spinach puree
- Salt to taste
- 1 tsp black pepper
- 2 tbsp mayonnaise
- 1 tsp paprika

Steps to Cook

1. First, take a pan and put it on medium heat. Then place the sandwich bread over the pan and toss the bread from both sides.

2. Take a food processor and add boiled chickpea, spinach puree, salt, black pepper, and paprika. Take a pan and heat some oil in it. Make small balls of it and fry it. Now spread mayonnaise on sandwich bread. Then add falafel balls, cucumber slices, tomato slices, red cabbage, avocado, and celery on sandwich bread.

3. Serve a falafel sandwich immediately. Enjoy!

Chapter 12: Sandwich Recipes

12.12 Jackfruit BBQ Sandwich

TIME TO PREPARE

10 minutes

COOK TIME

10 minutes

SERVING

4 people

Nutritional Facts

134 kcal

35 gr Prot.

Ingredients

- 2 bran burger bun
- 1 cup jackfruit shredded
- ¼ cup BBQ sauce
- Salt to taste
- 1 tsp vinegar
- ¼ cup carrot slices
- ¼ cup onion slices
- ½ cup mayonnaise
- 1 cup shredded red and plain cabbage
- 1 tbsp oil

Steps to Cook

1. First, take a pan and put it on medium heat. Then place the burger bun over the pan and toss the burger bun on both sides.

2. Now take another pan and heat some oil in it. Then add shredded jackfruit, salt, BBQ sauce, vinegar, onion, and carrot slices and cook it for 10 minutes. Put it aside.

3. Take another bowl and mix shredded cabbage with mayo.

4. Now assemble the Jackfruit BBQ sandwich by putting the jackfruit mixture above the bun and then adding shredded cabbage mixture and covering it with the other side of the bun. Serve the Jackfruit BBQ sandwich hot. Enjoy!

12.13 Grilled Eggplant Sandwich

TIME TO PREPARE
10 minutes

COOK TIME
10 minutes

SERVING
4 people

Nutritional Facts
155 kcal
27 gr Prot.

Ingredients

- 2 bran bread slices
- 2–3 spinach leaves
- 2 tbsp celery
- 2–3 eggplant, cut into slices
- Salt to taste
- 1 tsp paprika
- 1 tsp oil
- Vegan mayonnaise

Steps to Cook

1. First, take a pan and put it on medium heat. Then place bread slices over the pan and toss bread slices on both sides.

2. Now take a grilling pan and grease it with olive oil. Then, place eggplant in it and grill it on both sides. Take vegan mayonnaise and spread it on both sides of the bread. Then place grilled eggplant, spinach leaves, and celery. Sprinkle some salt and black pepper.

3. Then place the other bread slice over it and gently press it and then cut the grilled eggplant sandwich in half with the help of a knife. Serve it immediately. Enjoy!

Chapter 12: Sandwich Recipes

12.14 Vegetable Club Sandwich

TIME TO PREPARE
10 minutes

COOK TIME
10 minutes

SERVING
4 people

Nutritional Facts
157 kcal
30 gr Prot.

Ingredients

- 3 bran bread slices
- 2–3 lettuce leaves
- 4–6 tomato slices
- 4–6 cucumber slices
- 3–4 deli slices
- 1 cup boiled potato sliced
- 2 tbsp mayonnaise

Steps to Cook

1. First, take a pan and put it on medium heat. Then place bread slices over the pan and toss bread slices on both sides.

2. Now, spread mayonnaise on 3 slices of bread. Then add lettuce leaves and tomato boiled potato on the first layer and cover with bread slice. Now place the deli slice and cucumber over the second layer.

3. Then place the other bread slice over it and gently press it and then cut the vegetable club sandwich in half with the help of a knife. Serve it immediately. Enjoy!

Chapter 12: Sandwich Recipes

12.15 Grilled Spinach Cheese Sandwich

TIME TO PREPARE

10 minutes

COOK TIME

10 minutes

SERVING

4 people

Nutritional Facts

166 kcal

30 gr Prot.

Ingredients

- 2 bran bread slices
- ½ cup spinach leaves
- 1 cup low-fat cheese
- Salt to taste
- 1 tsp black pepper
- 1 tsp paprika
- 1 tsp olive oil

Steps to Cook

1. First, take a grilling pan and put it on medium heat. Then grease it with olive oil.

2. Now take a bread slice and spread spinach leaves over it. Then add vegan cheese over it. Sprinkle salt, black pepper, and paprika over it.

3. Then place the other bread slice over it and gently press it.

4. Place spinach sandwich into grilling pan and grill it on both sides until it shows marks. Then cut the grilled spinach sandwich in half with the help of a knife.

5. Serve it hot. Enjoy!

Chapter 12: Sandwich Recipes

12.16 Lentil Sandwich

TIME TO PREPARE
10 minutes

COOK TIME
10 minutes

SERVING
4 people

Nutritional Facts
175 kcal
30 gr Prot.

Ingredients

- 2 bran bread slices
- 2–3 iceberg leaves
- 4–6 tomato slices
- Cucumber slices
- Salt to taste
- 1 tsp black pepper
- ½ cup boiled lentils
- 1 tsp lemon juice

Steps to Cook

1. First, take a pan and put it on medium heat. Then place bread slices over the pan and toss bread slices from both sides.
2. Now take a bowl and add boiled lentils. Then add salt, black pepper, and lemon juice and mix it well. Take a bread slice and add iceberg, tomato slices, cucumber slices, and lentils over.
3. Then place the other bread slice over it, gently press it, and then cut the lentil sandwich in half with the help of a knife. Serve it immediately. Enjoy!

Chapter 12: Sandwich Recipes

12.17 Flaxseed Bread Salad Sandwich

TIME TO PREPARE

10 minutes

COOK TIME

10 minutes

SERVING

4 people

Nutritional Facts

157 kcal

25 gr Prot.

Ingredients

- Flaxseed bread slices
- Cucumber slices as required
- 4–5 avocado slices
- 2 tbsp vegan mayonnaise
- ¼ cup iceberg
- 4–6 red reddish, cut into slices
- ¼ cup mint leaves
- 1 tsp lemon juice

Steps to Cook

1. First, take a pan and put it on medium heat. Then place flaxseed bread slices over the pan and toss the bread slices on both sides.

2. Now spread mayonnaise on both slices of bread. Take a bowl and add all vegetables like spinach, cucumber, avocado, iceberg, reddish, and mint leaves, and then add lemon juice and mix it well. Spread it on one bread slice.

3. Then place the other bread slice over it, gently press it, and then cut the green flaxseed bread sandwich in half with the help of a knife. Serve it immediately. Enjoy!

12.18 Beetroot Patty Sandwich

TIME TO PREPARE
10 minutes

COOK TIME
10 minutes

SERVING
4 people

Nutritional Facts
145 kcal
30 gr Prot.

Ingredients

- 2 bran burger bun
- 2–3 spinach leaves
- 4–6 cumber slices
- 2–3 tomato slices
- 4–6 onion rings
- Salt to taste
- 1 tsp black pepper
- 1 tsp paprika
- 1 tsp oil
- 1 cup boiled beetroot
- 2 tbsp mayonnaise

Steps to Cook

1. First, take a pan and put it on medium heat. Then place the burger bun over the pan and toss it on both sides.

2. Take a food processor and add boiled beetroot, salt, black pepper, and paprika and mix it well. Make patties of it. Heat the oil in the pan and fry the beetroot patties on both sides until they turn golden brown.

3. Take the burger bun and spread mayonnaise. Then place beetroot patty, spinach, tomato, onion rings, and cucumber over it. Then cover it with the other side of the burger bun.

4. Serve it hot. Enjoy!

Chapter 12: Sandwich Recipes

12.19 Chickpea Patty Sandwich

TIME TO PREPARE

10 minutes

COOK TIME

10 minutes

SERVING

4 people

Nutritional Facts

156 kcal

30 gr Prot.

Ingredients

- 2 bran burger bun
- 2 3 spinach leaves
- 4–6 cucumber slices
- 2–3 avocado slices
- ¼ cup iceberg
- 2 tbsp coriander
- 2 tbsp mint
- Salt to taste
- 1 tsp black pepper
- 1 tsp paprika
- 1 tsp oil
- 2 tbsp vegan mayonnaise
- 1 cup boiled chickpeas

Steps to Cook

1. First, take a pan and put it on medium heat. Then place the burger bun over the pan and toss it on both sides.

2. Take a food processor and add boiled chickpea, coriander, mint, salt, black pepper, and paprika and mix it well. Make patties of it. Heat the oil in a pan and fry the chickpea patties on both sides until they turn golden brown.

3. Take the burger bun and spread vegan mayonnaise. Then place chickpea patty, spinach, avocado, iceberg, and cucumber over it. Then cover it with the other side of the bun.

4. Serve it hot. Enjoy!

Chapter 12: Sandwich Recipes

12.20 Grilled Tomato Sandwich

TIME TO PREPARE

10 minutes

COOK TIME

10 minutes

SERVING

4 people

Nutritional Facts

145 kcal

25 gr Prot.

Ingredients

- 2 bran bread slices
- 5–6 spinach leaves
- 4–6 tomato slices
- Salt to taste
- 1 tsp black pepper
- 1 cup low-fat cheese
- 2 tbsp mayonnaise
- 1 tsp vegetable oil

Steps to Cook

1. First, take a grilling pan and grease it with oil. Then place tomato slices over it and grill them on medium heat. Season with salt and black pepper.

2. Now spread mayonnaise on both slices of bread. Then add grilled tomato slices, spinach, and cheese.

3. Then place the other bread slice over it, gently press it, and grill it on the grilling pan until it shows marks, then cut the grilled tomato sandwich in half with the help of a knife.

4. Serve it immediately. Enjoy!

Chapter 12: Sandwich Recipes

12.21 Grilled Chicken Sub

TIME TO PREPARE
10 minutes

COOK TIME
10 minutes

SERVING
4 people

Nutritional Facts
147 kcal
30 gr Prot.

Ingredients

- 4 bran bread slices
- ½ cup lettuce leaves
- ½ cup tomato slices
- 1 tsp olive oil
- 1 tbsp low-fat mayonnaise
- 4 chicken breasts
- Salt to taste
- 1 tbsp black pepper

Steps to Cook

1. First, take a mixing bowl and add chicken pieces, salt, and black pepper. Set it aside for a 1-hour marinade.

2. Then take the roasting pan and grease it with olive oil. Grill chicken pieces for 10 minutes until cooked through or lightly browned on both sides.

3. Now toss the bread slices and spread mayonnaise on them evenly.

4. Then place lettuce and tomato slices on one slice of bread. Then place chicken breast on it. Cover it with the other slice of the bread.

5. Serve grilled chicken sub hot. Enjoy!

Chapter 12: Sandwich Recipes

12.22 Body Reset Ultimate Sandwich

TIME TO PREPARE
10 minutes

COOK TIME
10 minutes

SERVING
4 people

Nutritional Facts
147 kcal
30 gr Prot.

Ingredients

- 4 bran bread slices
- ½ cup lettuce leaves
- ½ cup tomato slices
- 1 tbsp low-fat mayonnaise
- 1 cup pepperoni slices
- 4 cheese slices

Steps to Cook

1. First, toss the bread slices and spread mayonnaise on them evenly.
2. Then place lettuce, pepperoni slices, cheese slices, and tomato slices on one slice of bread. Cover it with the other slice of bread.
3. Serve the body reset ultimate sandwich hot.
4. Enjoy!

Chapter 12: Sandwich Recipes

12.23 Lean Protein Sandwich

TIME TO PREPARE
10 minutes

COOK TIME
10 minutes

SERVING
4 people

Nutritional Facts
147 kcal
25 gr Prot.

Ingredients

- 4 bran bread slices
- ½ cup lettuce leaves
- ½ cup tomato slices
- ½ cup cucumber slices
- 1 tsp olive oil
- 1 tbsp low-fat mayonnaise
- 1 lb minced chicken
- Salt to taste
- 1 tbsp black pepper

Steps to Cook

1. First, take a mixing bowl and add minced chicken, salt, and black pepper. Set it aside for a 1-hour marinade. Make them in patty form.

2. Then take the grilling pan and grease it with olive oil. Grill chicken patties for 10 minutes until they become cooked or turn light golden from both sides.

3. Now toss the bread slices and spread mayonnaise on them evenly.

4. Then place lettuce, cucumber slices, and tomato slices on one slice of bread. Then place the chicken patty on it. Cover it with the other slice of bread.

5. Serve the lean protein sandwich hot. Enjoy!

Chapter 12: Sandwich Recipes

12.24 Grilled Salmon Sandwich

TIME TO PREPARE
10 minutes

COOK TIME
10 minutes

SERVING
4 people

Nutritional Facts
147 kcal
30 gr Prot.

Ingredients

- 4 bran bread slices
- ½ cup lettuce leaves
- ⅓ cup tomato slices
- ½ cup cucumber slices
- 1 tsp olive oil
- 1 tbsp low-fat mayonnaise
- 4 salmon pieces
- Salt to taste
- 1 tbsp black pepper

Steps to Cook

1. First, take a mixing bowl and add salmon pieces, salt, and black pepper. Set it aside for a 1-hour marinade.

2. Then take a grilling pan and grease it with olive oil. Grill salmon patties for 10 minutes until they become cooked or turn light golden from both sides.

3. Now toss the bread slices and spread mayonnaise on them evenly.

4. Then place lettuce, cucumber slices, and tomato slices on one slice of bread. Then place the salmon pieces on it. Cover it with the other slice of bread.

5. Serve the grilled salmon sandwich hot. Enjoy!

Chapter 12: Sandwich Recipes

12.25 Tuna Sandwich

TIME TO PREPARE

10 minutes

COOK TIME

10 minutes

SERVING

4 people

Nutritional Facts

147 kcal

30 gr Prot.

Ingredients

- 4 bran bread slices
- 1 tsp lemon juice
- 1 cup boiled and shredded tuna
- Salt to taste
- 1 tsp black pepper
- ¼ cup chopped cucumber
- ½ cup chopped cabbage
- ¼ cup chopped green bell peppers
- 1 cup mayonnaise

Steps to Cook

1. First, take a pan and put it on medium heat. Then place the bread slices over the pan and toss them on both sides.
2. Now take a bowl and add shredded tuna, mayonnaise, cucumber, green bell peppers, and cabbage, and sprinkle salt, black pepper, and lemon juice over it. Mix it well. Spread it on one bread slice.
3. Then place the other bread slice over it, gently press it, and then cut the tuna sandwich into 4 pieces with the help of a knife. Serve it immediately. Enjoy!

Chapter 12: Sandwich Recipes

12.26 Panini Sandwich

TIME TO PREPARE
10 minutes

COOK TIME
10 minutes

SERVING
4 people

Nutritional Facts
147 kcal
30 gr Prot.

Ingredients

- 4 bran panini sandwich
- ½ cup lettuce leaves
- ½ cup tomato slices
- 1 tsp olive oil
- 1 tbsp low-fat mayonnaise
- 1 lb ham slices
- 4 cheese slices

Steps to Cook

1. First, toss the panini sandwich, cut it in half, and spread mayonnaise on it evenly.
2. Then place lettuce, ham slices, cheese slices, and tomato slices on one slice of bread. Cover it with the other slice of bread.
3. Serve the panini sandwich hot.
4. Enjoy!

Chapter 12: Sandwich Recipes

12.27 Egg Protein Sandwich

TIME TO PREPARE

10 minutes

COOK TIME

10 minutes

SERVING

4 people

Nutritional Facts

147 kcal

30 gr Prot.

Ingredients

- 4 bran bread slices
- ½ cup lettuce leaves
- ½ cup tomato slices
- 1 tsp olive oil
- 1 tbsp low-fat mayonnaise
- 4 eggs
- 4 cheese slices
- Salt to taste
- 1 tbsp black pepper

Steps to Cook

1. First, take a pan and add olive oil. Then add whisked eggs into the pan and mix them to make scrambled eggs. Then toss the bread slices and spread mayonnaise on them evenly.

2. Then place lettuce, scrambled egg, cheese slices, and tomato slices on one slice of bread. Sprinkle salt and pepper. Cover it with the other slice of bread.

3. Serve the egg protein sandwich hot.

4. Enjoy!

Chapter 12: Sandwich Recipes

12.28 Avocado Toast

TIME TO PREPARE
10 minutes

COOK TIME
10 minutes

SERVING
4 people

Nutritional Facts
147 kcal
30 gr Prot.

Ingredients	Steps to Cook

Ingredients

- 4 bran bread slices
- ½ cup cherry tomatoes
- Coriander leaves for garnish
- 4–5 avocados
- Salt to taste
- 2 boiled eggs, cut into slices
- 1 tsp black pepper
- 1 tsp lemon juice

Steps to Cook

1. Take a bowl and mash avocados in it properly.
2. Now add salt, black pepper, and lemon juice to the mashed avocado paste and mix it well.
3. Toss bread slices in the pan and spread avocado mixture over it and then add cherry tomatoes and egg slices over it and garnish it with coriander leaves.
4. Serve the avocado toast. Enjoy!

Chapter 12: Sandwich Recipes

12.29 Deviled Egg Sandwich

TIME TO PREPARE

10 minutes

COOK TIME

10 minutes

SERVING

4 people

Nutritional Facts

147 kcal

30 gr Prot.

Ingredients

- 4 eggs
- 8 grilled bacon slices
- 4 cheese slices
- Salt to taste
- Black pepper to taste

Steps to Cook

1. First, boil the eggs and peel them.
2. Cut the boiled eggs in half.
3. Then take one half of the boiled egg and place cheese slices and 2 bacon slices on it.
4. Cover it with the other side of the boiled egg to form a sandwich. Sprinkle salt and black pepper.
5. Serve egg bites.
6. Enjoy!

Chapter 12: Sandwich Recipes

12.30 Chicken Mayo Sandwich

TIME TO PREPARE
10 minutes

COOK TIME
10 minutes

SERVING
4 people

Nutritional Facts
147 kcal
30 gr Prot.

Ingredients	Steps to Cook

Ingredients

- 4 bran bread slices
- 1 tsp lemon juice
- 1 cup boiled and shredded chicken
- Salt to taste
- 1 tsp black pepper
- ¼ cup chopped cucumber
- ½ cup chopped cabbage
- ¼ cup chopped capsicum
- ¼ cup chopped green bell peppers
- 1 cup low-fat mayonnaise

Steps to Cook

1. First, take a pan and put it on medium heat. Then place bread slices over the pan and toss bread slices from both sides.

2. Now take a bowl and add shredded chicken, mayonnaise, cucumber, capsicum, green bell peppers, and cabbage, and sprinkle salt, black pepper, and lemon juice over it. Mix it well. Spread it on the bread slice.

3. Then place the other bread slice over it, gently press it, and then cut the chicken mayo sandwich into 4 pieces with the help of a knife. Serve it immediately. Enjoy!

Chapter 12: Sandwich Recipes

12.31 Low-Calorie Chicken Sandwich

**TIME TO
PREPARE**

10 minutes

**COOK
TIME**

10 minutes

SERVING

4 people

**Nutritional
Facts**

147 kcal

30 gr Prot.

Ingredients

- 4 bran bread slices
- 1 tsp lemon juice
- 1 cup boiled and shredded chicken
- Salt to taste
- 1 tsp black pepper
- ½ cup boiled eggs chopped
- 1 cup low-fat mayonnaise

Steps to Cook

1. First, take a pan and put it on medium heat. Then place bread slices over the pan and toss the bread slices on both sides.

2. Now take a bowl and add shredded chicken, boiled egg cubes, and low-fat mayonnaise, and sprinkle salt, black pepper, and lemon juice over it. Mix it very well. Spread it on one bread slice.

3. Then place the other bread slice over it, gently press it, and then cut the low-calorie chicken sandwich into 4 pieces with the help of a knife. Serve it immediately. Enjoy!

Chapter 12: Sandwich Recipes

12.32 Club Sandwich

TIME TO PREPARE
10 minutes

COOK TIME
10 minutes

SERVING
4 people

Nutritional Facts
147 kcal
30 gr Prot.

Ingredients

- 3 bran bread slices
- 2-3 lettuce leaves
- 4-6 tomato slices
- 4-6 cucumber slices
- 3-4 grilled chicken breast
- 1 cup boiled potato sliced
- 2 tbsp low-fat mayonnaise

Steps to Cook

1. First, take a pan and put it on medium heat. Then place bread slices over the pan and toss the bread slices on both sides.

2. Now spread mayonnaise on 3 slices of bread. Then add lettuce leaves, tomato, and boiled potato on a layer and cover with one bread slice. Now place grilled chicken breast and cucumber over the second layer.

3. Then place the other bread slice over it and gently press it and then cut the club sandwich in half with the help of a knife. Serve it immediately. Enjoy!

Chapter 12: Sandwich Recipes

12.33 Low-Fat Cheese Sandwich

**TIME TO
PREPARE**

10 minutes

**COOK
TIME**

10 minutes

SERVING

4 people

**Nutritional
Facts**

147 kcal

30 gr Prot.

Ingredients

- 4 slices of bran bread
- 1 tbsp butter
- 1 cup low-fat shredded mozzarella cheese

Steps to Cook

1. First, take a pan and grease it with butter. Melt it.
2. Then put one slice on it. Add shredded low-fat mozzarella cheese to the top of the slice.
3. Cover it with the other slice of bread. Then cover the pan and cook it on low heat until the cheese melts.
4. Take out the low-fat cheese sandwich on a platter and serve it hot.
5. Enjoy!

Chapter 12: Sandwich Recipes

12.34 Philly Cheesesteak Sandwich

TIME TO PREPARE
10 minutes

COOK TIME
10 minutes

SERVING
4 people

Nutritional Facts
147 kcal
35 gr Prot.

Ingredients

- 4 bran subs
- ½ cup lettuce leaves
- ½ cup tomato slices
- ½ cup cucumber slices
- 4 cheese slices
- 1 tsp olive oil
- 1 tbsp low-fat mayonnaise
- 1 lb small beef slices
- Salt to taste
- 1 tbsp black pepper
- ½ caramelized onion

Steps to Cook

1. First, take a mixing bowl and add beef slices, salt, and black pepper. Set it aside for a 1-hour marinade.
2. Then take a grilling pan and grease it with olive oil. Grill beef slices for 10 minutes until they become cooked or turn light golden on both sides.
3. Now toss the bread slices and spread mayonnaise on them evenly.
4. Then place lettuce, cheese slice, caramelized onion, cucumber slices, and tomato slices on one slice of bread. Then place cooked beef slices on it. Sprinkle with salt and pepper. Cover it with the other slice of bread.
5. Serve the Philly cheesesteak sandwich hot. Enjoy!

Chapter 12: Sandwich Recipes

12.35 Mushroom Sub

TIME TO PREPARE

10 minutes

COOK TIME

10 minutes

SERVING

4 people

Nutritional Facts

147 kcal

35 gr Prot.

Ingredients

- 2 bran bread sub roll
- Salt to taste
- 1 tsp black pepper
- 1 tsp vinegar
- 1 tsp paprika powder
- 1 cup mushrooms
- 1 cup low-fat cheese
- 1 tsp vegetable oil
- ½ cup green bell peppers slices

Steps to Cook

1. First, take a pan and put it on medium heat. Then place bread sub roll over the pan and toss on both sides. Cut the sub from the center.

2. Now take a pan and put oil in it and place it on medium heat. Then add mushrooms and sauté for 5 minutes. Add salt, black pepper, vinegar, and paprika and mix it well. Then add green bell pepper slices and cheese and sauté for 2 minutes.

3. Then place the mushroom mixture in the bread sub roll and press it slightly. Serve it immediately. Enjoy!

Chapter 12: Sandwich Recipes

12.36 Turkey Sandwich

TIME TO PREPARE

10 minutes

COOK TIME

10 minutes

SERVING

4 people

Nutritional Facts

147 kcal

30 gr Prot.

Ingredients	Steps to Cook
• 4 bran bread slices • ½ cup lettuce leaves • ½ cup tomato slices • ½ cup cucumber slices • 1 tsp olive oil • 1 tbsp low-fat mayonnaise • 1 lb turkey sausages	1. Take a grilling pan and grease it with olive oil. Grill turkey sausages for 5 minutes. 2. Now toss the bread slices and spread mayonnaise on them evenly. 3. Then place lettuce, cucumber slices, and tomato slices on one slice of bread. Then place turkey on it. Cover it with the other slice of bread. 4. Serve turkey sandwich hot. Enjoy!

Chapter 12: Sandwich Recipes

12.37 Smoked Salmon Sandwich

TIME TO PREPARE
10 minutes

COOK TIME
10 minutes

SERVING
4 people

Nutritional Facts
147 kcal
30 gr Prot.

Ingredients

- 4 bran bread slices
- 1 tsp lemon juice
- 1 cup salmon slices
- Salt to taste
- 1 tsp black pepper
- ¼ cup chopped cucumber
- ½ cup chopped cabbage
- ¼ cup chopped capsicum
- ¼ cup chopped green bell peppers
- 1 cup low-fat mayonnaise

Steps to Cook

1. First, take a pan and put it on medium heat. Then place bread slices over the pan and toss them on both sides.

2. Now take a bowl and add mayonnaise, cucumber, capsicum, green bell peppers, and cabbage, and sprinkle salt, black pepper, and lemon juice over it. Mix it well. Spread it on one bread slice and then add salmon slices on top.

3. Then place the other bread slice over it, gently press it, and then cut the smoked salmon sandwich into 4 pieces with the help of a knife. Serve it immediately. Enjoy!

Chapter 12: Sandwich Recipes

12.38 Chicken Salad Sandwich

TIME TO PREPARE
10 minutes

COOK TIME
10 minutes

SERVING
4 people

Nutritional Facts
147 kcal
30 gr Prot.

Ingredients

- 4 bran bread slices
- 1 tsp lemon juice
- 1 cup boiled and shredded chicken
- Salt to taste
- 1 tsp black pepper
- ¼ cup chopped cucumber
- ¼ cup chopped tomatoes
- ¼ cup chopped onion
- ½ cup chopped cabbage
- ¼ cup chopped capsicum
- ¼ cup chopped green bell peppers

Steps to Cook

1. First, take a pan and put it on medium heat. Then place bread slices over the pan and toss them on both sides.

2. Now take a bowl and add shredded chicken, onion, tomatoes, cucumber, capsicum, green bell peppers, and cabbage, and sprinkle salt, black pepper, and lemon juice over it. Mix it well. Spread it on one bread slice.

3. Then place the other bread slice over it, gently press it, and then cut the chicken salad sandwich into 4 pieces with the help of a knife. Serve it immediately. Enjoy!

Chapter 12: Sandwich Recipes

12.39 Smoked Tuna Sandwich

TIME TO PREPARE

10 minutes

COOK TIME

10 minutes

SERVING

4 people

Nutritional Facts

147 kcal

30 gr Prot.

Ingredients

- 4 bran bread slices
- ½ cup lettuce leaves
- ½ cup tomato slices
- ½ cup cucumber slices
- 4 cheese slices
- 1 tsp olive oil
- 1 tbsp low-fat mayonnaise
- 1 lb tuna steak pieces
- Salt to taste
- 1 tbsp black pepper
- Caramelized onion

Steps to Cook

1. First, take a mixing bowl and add tuna steak pieces, salt, and black pepper. Set it aside for a 1-hour marinade.

2. Then take a grilling pan and grease it with olive oil. Grill tuna slices for 10 minutes until they become cooked or turn light golden from both sides.

3. Now spread mayonnaise on bread slices evenly.

4. Then place lettuce, cheese slice, caramelized onion, cucumber slices, and tomato slices on one slice of bread. Then place tuna slices on it. Cover it with the other slice of bread. Grill the sandwich for 5 minutes on both sides.

5. Serve the smoked tuna sandwich hot. Enjoy!

Chapter 12: Sandwich Recipes

12.40 Shrimp Meat Sandwich

TIME TO PREPARE

10 minutes

COOK TIME

10 minutes

SERVING

4 people

Nutritional Facts

147 kcal

30 gr Prot.

Ingredients

- 4 bread slices
- 1 tsp lemon juice
- 1 cup chopped grilled shrimps
- Salt to taste
- 1 tsp black pepper
- ¼ cup chopped cucumber
- ½ cup chopped cabbage
- ¼ cup chopped capsicum
- ¼ cup chopped green bell peppers
- 1 cup low-fat mayonnaise

Steps to Cook

1. First, take a pan and put it on medium heat. Then place bread slices over the pan and toss them on both sides.

2. Now take a bowl and add chopped grilled shrimps, mayonnaise, cucumber, capsicum, green bell peppers, and cabbage, and sprinkle salt, black pepper, and lemon juice over it. Mix it well. Spread it
on one bread slice.

3. Then place the other bread slice over it, gently press it, and then cut the shrimp meat sandwich into 4 pieces with the help of a knife. Serve it immediately. Enjoy!

Chapter 13:
Breakfast Recipes for Whole Body Reset Diet

Chapter 13: Breakfast Recipes

13.1 Chia Chocolate Smoothie Breakfast Bowl

TIME TO PREPARE
10 minutes

COOK TIME
10 minutes

SERVING
4 people

Nutritional Facts
147 kcal
25 gr Prot.

Ingredients

- 100 g fat-free yogurt
- 50 g chia seeds
- 1 tbsp choco powder
- 50 ml fat-free milk
- 2 banana
- 1 tbsp maple syrup
- Chocolate syrup for garnish

Steps to Cook

1. Take some milk in a glass and add chia seeds to it and soak it for overnight in a refrigerator.
2. Then take a blender and add fat-free yogurt, soaked chia seeds in milk, choco powder, banana, and maple syrup in it and blend it well.
3. Take out the chocolate chia smoothie in a bowl and garnish it with chocolate syrup and banana slices. Serve. Enjoy!

Chapter 13: Breakfast Recipes

13.2 Granola and Yogurt Breakfast Bowl

TIME TO PREPARE

10 minutes

COOK TIME

10 minutes

SERVING

4 people

Nutritional Facts

157 kcal

25 gr Prot.

Ingredients

- 100 g fat-free yogurt
- 50 g granola
- 50 g apple cubes

Steps to Cook

1. Take a bowl and add the fat-free yogurt. Mix it well.

2. Then add granola over the Greek yogurt and mix it slightly.

3. Add apple cubes to the top of the bowl. Serve the granola and yogurt bowl for breakfast. Enjoy!

Chapter 13: Breakfast Recipes

13.3 Strawberry Banana Smoothie Bowl

TIME TO PREPARE
10 minutes

COOK TIME
10 minutes

SERVING
4 people

Nutritional Facts
134 kcal
25 gr Prot.

Ingredients

- 100 g fat-free yogurt
- 50 g strawberries
- 2 banana
- Chocolate chips for garnish

Steps to Cook

1. Take a blender and add fat-free yogurt, strawberries, and banana and blend it well.

2. Take out the strawberry banana smoothie in a bowl and garnish it with chocolate chips, strawberries, and banana slices. Serve. Enjoy!

Chapter 13: Breakfast Recipes

13.4 Kiwi Smoothie Breakfast Bowl

**TIME TO
PREPARE**
10 minutes

**COOK
TIME**
10 minutes

SERVING
4 people

**Nutritional
Facts**
134 kcal
25 gr Prot.

Ingredients

- 100 g fat-free yogurt
- 50 g kiwi
- 2 banana
- 1 tbsp maple syrup

Steps to Cook

1. Take a blender and add fat-free yogurt, kiwi, banana, maple syrup in it and blend it very well.
2. Take out the kiwi banana smoothie in a bowl and garnish it with chocolate chips, raspberries, kiwi, and banana slices.
3. Serve. Enjoy!

Chapter 13: Breakfast Recipes

13.5 Blueberry Porridge Bowl

TIME TO PREPARE

10 minutes

COOK TIME

10 minutes

SERVING

4 people

Nutritional Facts

134 kcal

25 gr Prot.

Ingredients

- 50 ml fat-free milk
- 50 g blueberries
- 50 g porridge
- 50 g strawberries
- 2 banana
- Almonds for garnish
- Maple syrup

Steps to Cook

1. Take a bowl and add fat-free milk, maple syrup, and porridge in it. Cover it and put it aside for overnight to soak in the refrigerator.
2. Take this bowl out in the morning and top it with blueberries, strawberries, bananas, and almonds.
3. Serve the blueberry porridge bowl for breakfast. Enjoy!

Chapter 13: Breakfast Recipes

13.6 Acai Bowl

TIME TO PREPARE

10 minutes

COOK TIME

10 minutes

SERVING

4 people

Nutritional Facts

144 kcal

25 gr Prot.

Ingredients

- 50 ml fat-free milk
- 50 g blueberries
- 50 g strawberries
- 100 g frozen acai puree
- 100 g fat-free yogurt
- Raspberries, almonds, and chocolate chips to garnish

Steps to Cook

1. Take a blender and add fat-free milk, fat-free yogurt, blueberries, strawberries, frozen acai puree, and blend it well.
2. Take out the acai breakfast bowl in a bowl and garnish it with chocolate chips, raspberries, almonds, and blueberries.
3. Serve. Enjoy!

Chapter 13: Breakfast Recipes

13.7 Peanut Butter Banana Smoothie Bowl

TIME TO PREPARE

10 minutes

COOK TIME

10 minutes

SERVING

4 people

Nutritional Facts

174 kcal

27 gr Prot.

Ingredients

- 100 g fat-free yogurt
- 2 tbsp peanut butter
- 2 banana
- Chocolate chips to garnish

Steps to Cook

1. Take a blender and add fat-free yogurt, peanut butter, and banana and blend it well.

2. Take out the peanut butter banana smoothie in a bowl and garnish it with chocolate chips and banana slices.

3. Serve. Enjoy!

Chapter 13: Breakfast Recipes

13.8 Fruits and Oatmeal Breakfast Bowl

TIME TO PREPARE

10 minutes

COOK TIME

10 minutes

SERVING

4 people

Nutritional Facts

127 kcal

25 gr Prot.

Ingredients

- 50 g oats
- 50 g strawberries
- 50 ml fat-free yogurt
- 2 banana
- 50 g cherries
- Chocolate chips for garnish

Steps to Cook

1. Take a bowl and add oats on one side of the bowl and fat-free Yogurt on the other side.

2. Add strawberries, banana slices, cherries, and

   chocolate chips on top. Mix it well.

3. Serve the fruits and oatmeal bowl for breakfast. Enjoy!

Chapter 13: Breakfast Recipes

13.9 Guacamole and Egg

TIME TO PREPARE

10 minutes

COOK TIME

10 minutes

SERVING

4 people

Nutritional Facts

134 kcal

27 gr Prot.

Ingredients

- 1 tbsp olive oil
- 1 tsp lemon juice
- Salt to taste
- 2 avocado
- 100 g brown rice boiled
- 2 eggs
- 2 tbsp oil
- Bacon slices for garnish

Steps to Cook

1. First, take some oil in a pan and half fry the eggs.

2. Then take a small bowl and add avocadoes, salt, lemon juice, and olive oil. Mash it with the help of a masher and put it aside.

3. Now take a bowl and add brown rice. Top it with fried eggs and guacamole paste on one side.

4. Garnish it with bacon slices. Serve guacamole and egg bowl at breakfast. Enjoy!

Chapter 13: Breakfast Recipes

13.10 Egg Shakshuka

TIME TO PREPARE

10 minutes

COOK TIME

10 minutes

SERVING

4 people

Nutritional Facts

134 kcal

30 gr Prot.

Ingredients

- 1 tbsp olive oil
- Salt to taste
- Black pepper to taste
- 4 tbsp onion paste
- 6 tbsp tomato paste
- 2 eggs
- Parsley for garnish

Steps to Cook

1. Take a frying pan and heat oil in it. Then add onion paste and brown in it.

2. Then add tomato paste and mix it well.

3. Add salt and black pepper to the above mixture and mix it again.

4. Then break 2 eggs over the tomato paste and cover the pan and cook for 5 minutes.

5. Garnish it with parsley and serve it for breakfast. Enjoy!

Chapter 14:
Lunch Recipes for Whole Body Reset Diet

Chapter 14: Lunch Recipes

14.1 Rosemary Grilled Salmon

TIME TO PREPARE
10 minutes

COOK TIME
10 minutes

SERVING
4 people

Nutritional Facts
157 kcal
30 gr Prot.

Ingredients

- 6 oz salmon fillet
- 2 tbsp lemon juice
- 2 tbsp olive oil
- 1 tbsp rosemary, finely chopped
- 1 tbsp thyme, finely chopped
- 1 tsp red chili flakes
- 1 tsp each of salt and black pepper

Steps to Cook

1. In a small bowl, add lemon juice, rosemary, thyme, salt, black pepper, and red chili flakes, and stir well.

2. Pour this mixture into the salmon fillet and rub each side with clean hands. Set aside for 15–20 minutes.

3. In a pan heat the oil. Place the salmon on it and cook each side for 3–5 minutes or until light brown.

4. Transfer to a plate and garnish with a rosemary sprig.

5. Enjoy!

Chapter 14: Lunch Recipes

14.2 Dijon Baked Salmon

**TIME TO
PREPARE**

10 minutes

**COOK
TIME**

10 minutes

SERVING

4 people

**Nutritional
Facts**

155 kcal
30 gr Prot.

Ingredients

- 1 lb sockeye salmon
- ¼ cup fresh parsley, finely chopped
- ¼ cup Dijon mustard
- 1 tbsp lemon juice
- 1 tbsp avocado oil
- 3 garlic cloves, finely chopped
- Salt and pepper

Steps to Cook

1. Take a large bowl and mix the mustard, parsley, salt, pepper, lemon juice, oil, and garlic in it. Mix it well.

2. Then place the salmon on a parchment lined baking tray and give a generous coat the top of the salmon with the herbed mustard mix. Rub it with your hands. Set aside for 1 hour for marination.

3. Then bake the salmon in the oven for 20 minutes until it become properly cooked or changes its color to light brown. Serve it hot with sauteed vegetables and potato wedges. Enjoy!

Chapter 14: Lunch Recipes

14.3 Zucchini Noodles With Shrimp

TIME TO PREPARE

10 minutes

COOK TIME

10 minutes

SERVING

4 people

Nutritional Facts

133 kcal

30 gr Prot.

Ingredients

- 3 medium spiralized zucchinis
- 1 lb shrimps, peeled, and deveined
- 3 garlic cloves, chopped
- 1 tbsp lemon juice
- 1 tsp lemon zest
- 1 shallot, chopped
- 1 tsp each of salt and black pepper
- 2 tbsp avocado oil

Steps to Cook

1. Take a large pan and heat the oil. Add garlic, shrimps, shallot, salt, and black pepper. Stir to mix and cook per side for about 3–5 minutes until it turns pink. Remove from the pan to the plate.

2. In the same pan pour the remaining oil, add zucchini noodles in it, and season with salt and black pepper.

3. Add shrimps, lemon juice, and zest. Toss for about 1 minute.

4. Place on the plate and garnish it.

5. Serve warm.

Chapter 14: Lunch Recipes

14.4 Buttery Garlic Shrimps

TIME TO PREPARE

10 minutes

COOK TIME

10 minutes

SERVING

4 people

Nutritional Facts

145 kcal

30 gr Prot.

Ingredients

- 250 g shrimps
- 3 garlic cloves,finely chopped
- 1 tsp each of salt and black pepper
- 2 tbsp butter
- 1 tbsp lemon juice
- 2 tbsp parsley, chopped
- 1 tsp oregano

Steps to Cook

1. In a pan melt the butter, then add garlic and stir for 30 seconds. Then add in shrimps and sauté until it changes its color.
2. Then season with salt and black pepper and sprinkle your favorite herb oregano. Then add in lemon juice and stir for 3–5 minutes.
3. Transfer into a plate. Garnish with fresh parsley and serve hot with garlic rice.
4. Serve it. Enjoy!

Chapter 14: Lunch Recipes

14.5 Smoked Trout

TIME TO PREPARE

10 minutes

COOK TIME

10 minutes

SERVING

4 people

Nutritional Facts

167 kcal

30 gr Prot.

Ingredients

- ½ kg trout fish
- 1 tbsp lemon juice
- 1 tsp chili powder
- 1 tsp chopped garlic
- 1 tsp chili flakes
- 1 tsp paprika
- Salt as required
- 1 tbsp butter

Steps to Cook

1. Take a small pan and add trout fish, lemon juice, chili powder, chopped garlic, chili flakes, paprika, and salt. Toss it well and set it aside for marination for at least 1 hour. Then place the marinated shrimps onto the skewers.

2. Then take a grilling pan and grease it with butter. Cook shrimps over it for 5–8 minutes with brushing with butter.

3. Take it out on a platter and serve the smoked trout hot. Enjoy!

Chapter 14: Lunch Recipes

14.6 Lemon Cod With Stir Fry Vegetables

TIME TO PREPARE

10 minutes

COOK TIME

10 minutes

SERVING

4 people

Nutritional Facts

145 kcal

30 gr Prot.

Ingredients

- 1 lb cod
- 1 tbsp paprika
- 1 tbsp rosemary
- Salt to taste
- 2 tsp black pepper
- 2 tsp garlic paste
- 2 tsp ginger paste
- 4 tbsp lemon juice

Steps to Cook

1. Take a bowl and add ginger and garlic paste, salt and black pepper, lemon juice, paprika, rosemary, and cod and mix them well with a spatula.
2. Now put this marinated cod over the grilling pan and grill it for 15 minutes.
3. Take out grilled codfish on a platter and serve it with sautéed vegetables. Enjoy!

Chapter 14: Lunch Recipes

14.7 Grilled Turkey Breast With Vegetables

TIME TO PREPARE

10 minutes

COOK TIME

10 minutes

SERVING

4 people

Nutritional Facts

144 kcal

30 gr Prot.

Ingredients

- 1 lb turkey breast
- 1 tbsp paprika
- 1 tbsp rosemary
- Salt to taste
- 2 tsp black pepper
- 2 tsp garlic paste
- 2 tsp ginger paste
- 4 tbsp lemon juice

Steps to Cook

1. Take a bowl and add ginger and garlic paste, salt and black pepper, lemon juice, paprika, rosemary, and turkey and mix them well with a spatula.

2. Now put this marinated turkey over the grilling pan and grill it for 15 minutes.

3. Take out the grilled turkey on a platter and serve it with sautéed vegetables. Enjoy!

14.8 Grilled Lobster Tails

TIME TO PREPARE

10 minutes

COOK TIME

10 minutes

SERVING

4 people

Nutritional Facts

147 kcal

30 gr Prot.

Ingredients

- 6 lobster tails
- ¾ cup avocado oil
- 3 tbsp chives, minced
- 3 garlic cloves, mince
- Salt and pepper to taste

Steps to Cook

1. Take a large bowl and add lobster tails with fresh minced chives, garlic cloves, salt, and black pepper. Set aside for marination for at least 1 hour.

2. Now take a grilling pan and grease it with avocado oil. Add the above marinated lobster tails into the grilling pan and grill it on both sides for about 10 minutes. Take it out in platter. Serve it hot. Enjoy!

14.9 Lemon Grilled Chicken

TIME TO PREPARE

10 minutes

COOK TIME

10 minutes

SERVING

4 people

Nutritional Facts

145 kcal

30 gr Prot.

Ingredients

- ½ kg boneless chicken breast
- Salt to taste
- 1 tsp black pepper
- 1 tbsp vinegar
- 1 tbsp soy sauce
- 1 tbsp extra-virgin olive oil
- 1 tsp garlic paste
- 1 tsp ginger paste
- 2 tbsp lemon juice
- Lemon slices

Steps to Cook

1. Take a bowl and add chicken breast, soya sauce, vinegar, lemon juice, ginger, garlic paste, salt, and black pepper and mix them well with a spatula.
2. Now marinate the chicken breast for 1 hour.
3. Now take a grilling pan, heat oil, and put lemon slices over the grilling pan. Then place the chicken breast pieces above the lemon slices and grill for 15 minutes until they become properly cooked on both sides and they turn light golden. Serve it hot. You can serve it with mint yogurt.

14.10 Grilled Tuna Steak

TIME TO PREPARE
10 minutes

COOK TIME
10 minutes

SERVING
4 people

Nutritional Facts
167 kcal
30 gr Prot.

Ingredients

- 1 lb tuna steak pieces
- Salt to taste
- 1 tbsp black pepper
- 1 tbsp lemon juice
- 1 tbsp olive oil

Steps to Cook

1. Take a bowl and add tuna steak, salt, black pepper, and lemon juice. Mix it very well.
2. Marinate it for at least 1 hour.
3. Then take a grilling pan and grease it with olive oil.
4. Put the tuna steak in it and grill it on both sides until it turns brown.
5. Serve it hot. Enjoy!

Chapter 15:
Snack Recipes for Whole Body Reset Diet

Chapter 15: Snack Recipes

15.1 Roasted Brussel Sprouts

TIME TO PREPARE
10 minutes

COOK TIME
10 minutes

SERVING
4 people

Nutritional Facts
117 kcal
15 gr Prot.

Ingredients	Steps to Cook

Ingredients

- 1 kg Brussels sprouts
- 1 tsp lemon juice
- Salt to taste
- 1 tbsp black pepper
- 1 tsp oregano
- 1 tsp thyme
- 1 tbsp olive oil
- 1 tbsp mustard sauce
- Cannabis leaves powder

Steps to Cook

1. Take Brussels sprouts and wash them properly with water.

2. Take a large bowl and add Brussels sprouts. Then add lemon juice, salt, black pepper, thyme, oregano, and cannabis leaves powder and mix well.

3. Heat baking oven and grease oven dish with olive oil. Put the Brussels sprout in the baking dish and bake it in the oven for 15 minutes until it turns golden brown and becomes crisp. Serve it for a snack. You can serve it with mustard sauce.

Chapter 15: Snack Recipes

15.2 Air-Fried Chicken Strips

TIME TO PREPARE

10 minutes

COOK TIME

10 minutes

SERVING

4 people

Nutritional Facts

134 kcal

27 gr Prot.

Ingredients

- 1 kg chicken strips
- 1 tsp lemon juice
- Salt to taste
- 1 tbsp black pepper
- 1 tsp oregano
- 1 tsp thyme
- 1 tbsp olive oil
- 1 tbsp mustard sauce
- 1 tbsp flour

Steps to Cook

1. Take chicken strips and wash them properly with water.
2. Take a large bowl and add chicken strips to it. Then add lemon juice, salt, black pepper, thyme, oregano, and flour in it and mix it well.
3. Heat the baking oven and grease the oven dish with olive oil. Put the chicken strips in the baking dish and bake them in the oven for 15 minutes until it turns golden brown and becomes crispy.
4. Serve it for a snack. You can serve it with mustard sauce.
5. You can also air-fry it.

Chapter 15: Snack Recipes

15.3 Protein Bars

TIME TO PREPARE
10 minutes

COOK TIME
10 minutes

SERVING
4 people

Nutritional Facts
144 kcal
28 gr Prot.

Ingredients

- ¾ cup almond butter
- ⅓ cup Monk Fruit
- 2 tbsp coconut oil
- 2 cups rolled oats
- 2 scoops vanilla protein powder
- 3 tbsp flaxseed meal
- ¼ tsp ground cinnamon
- ¼ tsp salt
- ⅓ cup dark chocolate pieces
- ¼ cup nuts or as required

Steps to Cook

1. Place the almond butter, monk fruit sweetener, and coconut oil in a double boiler and melt it. Remove it from heat.
2. Then add the oats, protein powder, flaxseed, cinnamon, nuts, and salt. Mix them well, then stir in the dark chocolate chip pieces.
3. Press properly into the prepared pan and refrigerate the bars for 1 hour or until firm.
4. Slice the protein bars of desired sizes and serve. Enjoy!

Chapter 15: Snack Recipes

15.4 Deviled Eggs

TIME TO PREPARE
10 minutes

COOK TIME
10 minutes

SERVING
4 people

Nutritional Facts
117 kcal
28 gr Prot.

Ingredients

- 4 large eggs
- 3 tbsp mayonnaise
- 1 tsp Dijon mustard
- 1 tsp apple cider vinegar
- Salt and pepper to taste
- Paprika for garnish

Steps to Cook

1. Bring a pot of water to boil. Boil eggs in it.
2. After 14 minutes, remove the eggs from the water in the pot and place the eggs in an ice water bath.
3. Remove the yolk to a small bowl with the help of a spoon and place the egg whites on a plate.
4. Mash the yolks with the help of a fork and add your desire dressing - mayonnaise, mustard, vinegar, salt, and pepper - on the top of the eggs. Mix it properly.
5. Use a spoon to add a portion of the deviled egg mixture egg white.

Chapter 15: Snack Recipes

15.5 Fish Meat Balls

TIME TO PREPARE

10 minutes

COOK TIME

10 minutes

SERVING

4 people

Nutritional Facts

145 kcal

28 gr Prot.

Ingredients

- 500 g salmon, cut into cubes
- **3 tbsp** breadcrumbs
- ½ onion, chopped
- 1 egg
- 1 tsp salt
- 1 tsp black pepper
- 1 tsp lemon juice
- 1 garlic clove, minced
- ½ tsp oregano
- ½ tsp thyme
- Olive oil as required

Steps to Cook

1. Take a food processor, add salmon and chop finely.
2. Transfer this mixture into a bowl and add breadcrumbs, onion,

   salt, black pepper, lemon juice, garlic, oregano, thyme, and egg. Mix well with a clean hand and make small balls.
3. Preheat your oven to 350°F. Line the baking tray and grease it with butter.
4. Place prepared salmon balls and brush them with olive oil. Bake for about 13–15 minutes.
5. Transfer to a serving plate and serve with your favorite dip.

Chapter 15: Snack Recipes

15.6 Zucchini Muffins

TIME TO PREPARE
10 minutes

COOK TIME
10 minutes

SERVING
4 people

Nutritional Facts
145 kcal
22 gr Prot.

Ingredients

- 1 cup whole wheat flour
- ½ cup zucchini puree
- ¼ cup coconut oil
- 2 tbsp of dairy-free yogurt
- ½ cup liquid stevia
- 2 eggs
- 1 tsp cinnamon
- ½ tsp nutmeg
- ½ tsp cloves
- 1 tsp baking powder
- ½ tsp baking soda
- A pinch of salt
- ¼ tsp vanilla extract

Steps to Cook

1. Preheat your oven to 375°F and grease the muffin pan with coconut oil.
2. Take a large bowl and combine flour, baking powder cinnamon, cloves, baking soda, salt, and nutmeg and mix well with the whisker.
3. Take a small bowl, add zucchini puree, melted coconut oil, eggs vanilla extract, yogurt, and liquid stevia and mix with the whisker.
4. Combine the dry mixture with the wet mixture.
5. Transfer the batter with the help of a rounded tablespoonful into the muffin pan.
6. Bake for about 25–30 minutes in preheated oven and cool for 30 minutes. Eat and enjoy!

Chapter 15: Snack Recipes

15.7 Air-Fried Cauliflower Wings

TIME TO PREPARE
10 minutes

COOK TIME
10 minutes

SERVING
4 people

Nutritional Facts
156 kcal
23 gr Prot.

Ingredients

- 1 cauliflower head cut into bite-sized florets
- 2 tbsp avocado oil
- 1 tsp garlic powder
- 1 tsp salt
- ½ tsp black pepper
- 3 tbsp hot sauce
- 1 tbsp vinegar

Steps to Cook

1. Preheat the oven to 400°F.
2. Place the bite-sized cauliflower florets into the baking tray. Drizzle some avocado oil on them. Season with black pepper, salt, and garlic powder.
3. Bake for about 15 minutes, change the side and check the tenderness. Bake for about another 10 minutes for desired tenderness and crispiness. Remove from the oven.
4. To make the buffalo sauce, in a bowl mix hot sauce, vinegar, and salt. Melt the coconut oil and mix it.
5. Toss all the baked florets into the sauce and cook for 5–10 minutes. Serve with any dipping sauce.
6. You can also air-fry it.

Chapter 15: Snack Recipes

15.8 Zucchini Fries

TIME TO PREPARE
10 minutes

COOK TIME
10 minutes

SERVING
4 people

Nutritional Facts
117 kcal
20 gr Prot.

Ingredients

- 1 medium zucchini cut lengthwise
- ½ cup breadcrumbs
- ¼ cup flour
- ½ tsp salt
- ½ tsp black pepper
- ½ tsp garlic powder
- ¼ tsp onion powder

Steps to Cook

1. Preheat the oven up to 425°F. Line the baking tray with parchment paper.
2. Dry the zucchini strips properly.
3. On a large flat plate, mix breadcrumbs, black pepper, garlic powder, salt, and onion powder. Mix well with the fork.
4. In a shallow bowl make flour paste properly.
5. Dip the zucchini strips in the flour and then coat in the mixture of breadcrumbs and vegan cheese. Press properly to make sure it is completely coated. Repeat with the other zucchini strips.
6. Place the zucchini strip on a prepared baking tray and bake for about 25–30 minutes.
7. Sprinkle some parsley and serve hot.

Chapter 15: Snack Recipes

15.9 Oatmeal Walnut Cookies

TIME TO PREPARE

10 minutes

COOK TIME

10 minutes

SERVING

4 people

Nutritional Facts

147 kcal

22 gr Prot.

Ingredients	Steps to Cook
<ul><li>1 ½ cups flour</li><li>1 tsp baking soda</li><li>1 ½ tsp cinnamon</li><li>1 tsp salt</li><li>1 ¼ cups softened butter</li><li>¾ cup brown sugar, packed</li><li>2 tbsp egg substitute powder</li><li>1 tsp vanilla</li><li>3 cups rolled oats</li><li>1 ¼ cup walnuts chopped</li></ul>	1. Take a large bowl and combine the flour, baking soda, cinnamon, and salt in it. Set the bowl aside. 2. Take another bowl and add butter and brown sugar. Add the egg substitute and vanilla. Mix it well. Then, add the flour mixture to the above-prepared mixture. Stir in the oats and walnuts. 3. Make small balls of cookies. 4. Bake the cookies in the oven for 10–15 minutes until they turn light gold. 5. Take the oatmeal walnut cookies out from the oven and serve them hot.

Chapter 15: Snack Recipes

15.10 Guacamole Spread

TIME TO PREPARE
10 minutes

COOK TIME
10 minutes

SERVING
4 people

Nutritional Facts
123 kcal
20 gr Prot.

Ingredients

- 3 mashed avocados
- 1 lime, juiced
- 1 tsp salt
- ½ cup diced onion
- 3 tbsp chopped fresh cilantro
- 2 tomatoes, diced
- 1 tsp minced garlic
- A pinch of ground cayenne pepper (optional)

Steps to Cook

1. Take a bowl, add avocados, lime juice, and salt in it and mix it well.

2. Then add onion, cilantro, tomatoes, and garlic. Stir in cayenne pepper. Mix it well.

3. Serve it with pita bread triangles or nachos. Enjoy!

Chapter 16:
Dinner Recipes for Whole Body Reset Diet

Chapter 16: Dinner Recipes

16.1 Crab Cake

TIME TO PREPARE

10 minutes

COOK TIME

10 minutes

SERVING

4 people

Nutritional Facts

142 kcal

28 gr Prot.

Ingredients

- 2 green onions, finely chopped
- 1 large egg
- 1 tsp lemon juice
- Salt, pepper, cayenne, and garlic powder to taste
- ½ kg minced crab meat
- 1 tbsp butter

Steps to Cook

1. Take a food processor and add crab meat, salt, black pepper, cayenne pepper, garlic powder, lemon juice, and green onion and mix it. Make balls of it and give them the shape of a patty.

2. Take a bowl and beat eggs in it.

3. Coat crab cake with eggs.

4. Heat the butter in a non-stick pan and shallow fry the fish cake for 10 minutes until it becomes properly cooked and turns golden brown. Serve this hot for dinner. Enjoy!

16.2 Buttery Scallops

TIME TO PREPARE
10 minutes

COOK TIME
10 minutes

SERVING
4 people

Nutritional Facts
144 kcal
28 gr Prot.

Ingredients

- ½ kg scallops peeled and deveined
- 3 tbsp butter
- 2 tbsp lemon juice
- ½ tsp salt
- ¼ tsp pepper
- 1 tsp oregano
- ½ tsp paprika
- ½ tsp garlic powder
- Chopped parsley for serving
- Lemon slices for serving

Steps to Cook

1. First, take a large bowl and add butter, lemon juice, salt, pepper, oregano, paprika, and garlic powder and combine.
2. Then add the scallops to it and toss gently. Marinate for at least 1 hour.
3. Take wooden skewers and thread 4–6 scallops on each skewer.
4. Put the grilling pan on medium-high heat and cook the scallops for 10 minutes until it changes their color. Serve it hot. Enjoy!
5. Serve it with fresh parsley and lemon slices.

Chapter 16: Dinner Recipes

16.3 Spicy Red Snapper

TIME TO PREPARE

10 minutes

COOK TIME

10 minutes

SERVING

4 people

Nutritional Facts

143 kcal

30 gr Prot.

Ingredients

- 1 lb red snapper fish
- Salt to taste
- 2 tsp black pepper
- 2 tsp garlic paste
- 2 tsp ginger paste
- 4 tbsp lemon juice
- Lemon slices as required
- 1 tbsp butter
- 1 tbsp chopped garlic
- Parsley

Steps to Cook

1. Take a bowl and add ginger and garlic paste, salt, black pepper, lemon juice, and red snapper fish and mix them well with a spatula.
2. Now put this marinated snapper over the grilling pan and grill it for 15 minutes.
3. Now take a pan and add butter to it. Add chopped garlic and parsley to it. Cook it for 1 minute.
4. Pour this butter sauce over the grilled red snapper and serve it. Enjoy!

16.4 Salmon Noodles

TIME TO PREPARE

10 minutes

COOK TIME

10 minutes

SERVING

4 people

Nutritional Facts

145 kcal

30 gr Prot.

Ingredients

- 4–5 zucchini
- Salt to taste
- ½ cup chopped kale
- 1 tbsp black pepper
- 1 tbsp avocado oil
- Coriander leaves for garnish
- 1 tsp oregano
- 1lb shrimps
- ½ cup cherry tomatoes

Steps to Cook

1. First, take zucchini and cut them into strips like noodles with the help of a cutter or some peeler.
2. Take a saucepan and boil water in it and add zucchini noodles in it and boil for 10 minutes and remove the water properly from it.
3. Take a pan and put some avocado oil in it and add zucchini noodles and shrimps and stir fry for 5 minutes.
4. Now add salt, black pepper, oregano, and zucchini noodles and mix them well. Add kale and cherry tomatoes to it. Serve zucchini noodles hot for dinner. Garnish with coriander leaves. Enjoy!

Chapter 16: Dinner Recipes

16.5 Thai Prawns

TIME TO PREPARE

10 minutes

COOK TIME

10 minutes

SERVING

4 people

Nutritional Facts

156 kcal

30 gr Prot.

Ingredients

- 1 lb prawns
- 1 tbsp Thai seasoning
- ½ cup tomato paste
- ½ cup onion paste
- 2 tbsp vegetable oil
- Salt to taste
- 1 tbsp red chili powder
- 1 tbsp turmeric powder
- 1 tsp ginger garlic paste
- 5–6 green chilies
- ¼ cup coriander leaves
- 1 cup boiled rice

Steps to Cook

1. Take a pan and put some oil in it and heat it. Then add onion paste and cook it until it turns golden brown.
2. Now add ginger garlic paste to the above onion paste and further cook for 1 minute. Now add tomato paste and further cook it for 3 minutes.
3. Add prawns and add Thai seasoning, salt, red chili powder, turmeric powder, green chili, and coriander leaves and mix it well. Then cover it with a lid and cook it for further 10 minutes.
4. Take boiled rice on a platter and add Thai prawns with it and serve it hot at dinner.

16.6 Stir-Fried Chicken

**TIME TO
PREPARE**

10 minutes

**COOK
TIME**

10 minutes

SERVING

4 people

**Nutritional
Facts**

144 kcal

30 gr Prot.

Ingredients

- ½ kg bonelesschicken strips
- Salt to taste
- 1 tbsp black pepper
- 1 tbsp vinegar
- ¼ cup sliced red capsicum
- ¼ cup sliced green capsicum
- 1 tbsp avocado oil
- 2 tbsp red chili flakes

Steps to Cook

1. Take avocado oil in a pan and put it on medium heat, add chicken strips, salt, black pepper, and vinegar and cook them for 15 minutes.

2. Then add red and green capsicum and red chili flakes and further cook for 5 minutes.

3. Garnish the stir fry chicken and serve it. Enjoy!

Chapter 16: Dinner Recipes

16.7 Chicken Stew

TIME TO PREPARE

10 minutes

COOK TIME

10 minutes

SERVING

4 people

Nutritional Facts

134 kcal

30 gr Prot.

Ingredients

- 1 tbsp avocado oil
- 1 tbsp butter
- 1 medium onion diced
- 1 tbsp ginger garlic paste
- ½ kg boneless chicken
- 4 tbsp tomato paste
- 1 tbsp garam masala
- 1 tsp chili powder
- 1 tsp Fenugreek
- 1 tsp cumin
- 1 tsp salt
- ¼ tsp black pepper
- 1 cup coconut cream
- 1 cup boiled rice

Steps to Cook

1. First, take a pan and heat the avocado oil. Add ginger and garlic paste and sauté it for 5 minutes. Then add chopped onion and further cook for 5 minutes until the onion color changes to a golden brown.

2. After that add tomato paste to it. Add Fenugreek, cumin, black pepper, salt, garam masala, and chili powder and mix it well.

3. Add boneless chicken to it and mix it again. Cover it and cook for 15–20 minutes until the chicken becomes properly cooked. Add 1 cup coconut cream and 1 tbsp butter at the end. Mix it well again. Serve the chicken stew hot with boiled rice. Enjoy!

16.8 Rosemary Roasted Chicken

TIME TO PREPARE

10 minutes

COOK TIME

10 minutes

SERVING

4 people

Nutritional Facts

144 kcal

30 gr Prot.

Ingredients

- 1.1 lb chicken leg thighs
- 1 tbsp olive oil
- ¼ tsp salt
- ¼ tsp ground black pepper
- ¼ tsp dried oregano
- ¼ tsp dried basil
- ¼ tsp paprika
- 1 tbsp rosemary
- ⅛ tsp cayenne pepper

Steps to Cook

1. Put chicken thighs in a tray. Rub with olive oil. Mix the salt, pepper, oregano, basil, rosemary, paprika, and cayenne pepper, and toss by hand so all sides of the chicken will be well coated.

2. Preheat the baking oven to medium-high heat.

3. Take a baking dish and grease it with oil. Add marinated chicken thighs. Put it in the oven and roast for 20 minutes until the chicken changes its color from all sides. Take it on the serving platter and enjoy!

Chapter 16: Dinner Recipes

16.9 Chicken Fajita

TIME TO PREPARE

10 minutes

COOK TIME

10 minutes

SERVING

4 people

Nutritional Facts

143 kcal

30 gr Prot.

Ingredients

- ½ kg boneless chicken strips
- Salt to taste
- 1 tbsp black pepper
- 1 tbsp vinegar
- 1 tbsp tamari sauce
- 1 tbsp chili sauce
- ¼ cup sliced yellow capsicum
- 1 tbsp sugar-free ketchup
- ¼ cup sliced red capsicum
- ¼ cup sliced green capsicum
- 1 tbsp avocado oil
- 2 tbsp red chili flakes

Steps to Cook

4. Take the avocado oil into a pan and put it on medium heat, add chicken strips, salt, black pepper, vinegar, tamari sauce, chili sauce, and sugar-free ketchup and cook it for 15 minutes.
5. Then add red, yellow, and green capsicum and red chili flakes and further cook it for 5 minutes.
6. Garnish the chicken fajita and serve it. Enjoy!

16.10 Chicken Parmesan

TIME TO PREPARE
10 minutes

COOK TIME
10 minutes

SERVING
4 people

Nutritional Facts
134 kcal
30 gr Prot.

Ingredients

- 4 chicken breasts
- ½ cup flour
- 2 eggs
- ½ cup breadcrumbs
- Salt and black pepper to taste
- ½ cup Parmesan cheese grated
- 2 tbsp parsley
- 4 tbsp oil
- 1 tbsp marinara sauce
- 1 cup low-fat Mozzarella cheese shredded
- ¼ cup low-fat Parmesan cheese shredded
- Basil and parsley fresh, chopped

Steps to Cook

1. Combine breadcrumbs, grated Parmesan, fresh parsley, salt, and pepper to taste in a bowl.
2. Dip chicken into flour. Then dip the chicken in beaten eggs and then into the breadcrumb mixture.
3. Preheat some olive oil in a large pan. Brown chicken on each side, cooking it for about 4 minutes per side or until it turns golden brown in color.
4. Then place marinara sauce at the bottom of the dish. Add the browned chicken. Top each piece with a couple of spoons of Marinara sauce, Mozzarella, and sprinkle some Parmesan on the top.
5. Bake it for about 20–25 minutes or until golden. Sprinkle with fresh herbs and serve over pasta.
6. Serve it hot. Enjoy!

28-DAY MEAL PLAN
DURING THE MAINTENANCE PERIOD

	1st Day Plan
Breakfast	Flat Belly Cantaloupe Juice + 1 Sandwich
Shakes and soups	Creamy Tomato Soup
Lunch	Rosemary Grilled Salmon
Salad	Chicken Tomato Salad
Dinner	Lemon Grilled Chicken
Dessert Smoothie	Coconut Cashew Protein Smoothie
	2nd Day Plan
Breakfast	Super Green Juice + 1 Sandwich
Shakes and soups	Red Lentil Soup
Lunch	Grilled Tuna Steak
Salad	Body Reset Egg Salad
Dinner	Air Fryer Chicken Strips
Dessert Smoothie	Peach Cobbler
	3rd Day Plan
Breakfast	Carrot Juice + 1 Sandwich
Shakes and soups	Sweet Potato Soup
Lunch	Dijon Baked Salmon
Salad	Salmon Salad
Dinner	Deviled Eggs
Dessert Smoothie	Banana Split
	4th Day Plan
Breakfast	Flat Belly Pomegranate Juice + 1 Sandwich
Shakes and soups	Creamy Mushroom Soup
Lunch	Smoked Trout
Salad	Burrito Salad
Dinner	Zucchini Muffins
Dessert Smoothie	Kiwi Splash
	5th Day Plan
Breakfast	Watermelon Juice + 1 Sandwich
Shakes and soups	Raspberry Weight Loss Smoothie
Lunch	Avocado Sandwich
Salad	Quinoa Vegetable Salad

Dinner	Crab Cake
Dessert Smoothie	Almond Shake
6th Day Plan	
Breakfast	Beetroot Juice + 1 Sandwich
Shakes and soups	Roasted Carrot Soup
Lunch	Potato Patty Sandwich
Salad	Beans Salad
Dinner	Rosemary Roasted Chicken
Dessert Smoothie	Chocolate Nut Smoothie
7th Day Plan	
Breakfast	Orange Detox Juice + 1 Sandwich
Shakes and soups	Chocolate Nut Smoothie
Lunch	Buttery Garlic Shrimps
Salad	Chicken and Bulgur Salad Bowl
Dinner	Chicken Stew
Dessert Smoothie	Date Shake
8th Day Plan	
Breakfast	Tropical Carrot Apple Juice + 1 Sandwich
Shakes and soups	Kale Recharge Smoothie
Lunch	Lemon Cod with Stir Fry Vegetables
Salad	Brown Lentils Salad
Dinner	Buttery Scallops
Dessert Smoothie	Date Shake
9th Day Plan	
Breakfast	Chia Seeds Lemonade + 1 Sandwich
Shakes and soups	Pineapple Weight Loss Smoothie
Lunch	Grilled Turkey Breast with Vegetables
Salad	Tofu Berry Salad
Dinner	Chicken Parmesan
Dessert Smoothie	Coconut Cashew Protein Smoothie
10th Day Plan	
Breakfast	Grape Fruit Juice + 1 Sandwich
Shakes and soups	Almond Shake
Lunch	Grilled Lobster Tails
Salad	Chickpea Salad
Dinner	Stir-Fry Chicken
Dessert Smoothie	Kiwi Splash
11th Day Plan	
Breakfast	Blueberry Juice + 1 Sandwich
Shakes and soups	Banana Split

Lunch	Lemon Cod with Stir Fry Vegetables
Salad	Mango Kale Salad
Dinner	Chicken Fajita
Dessert Smoothie	Almond Shake
	12th Day Plan
Breakfast	Kiwi Splash + 1 Sandwich
Shakes and soups	Rosemary Grilled Salmon
Lunch	Grilled Tuna Steak
Salad	Body Reset Corn Salad
Dinner	Zucchini Muffins
Dessert Smoothie	Date Shake
	13th Day Plan
Breakfast	Raspberry Weight Loss Smoothie + 1 Sandwich
Shakes and soups	Peach Cobbler
Lunch	Smoked Trout
Salad	Red Beans and Chickpea Salad
Dinner	Chicken Parmesan
Dessert Smoothie	Banana Split
	14th Day Plan
Breakfast	Almond Shake + 1 Sandwich
Shakes and soups	Pumpkin Soup
Lunch	Lemon Grilled Chicken
Salad	Stuffed Avocado Salad
Dinner	Deviled Eggs
Dessert Smoothie	Chocolate Nut Smoothie
	15th Day Plan
Breakfast	Dates Shake + 1 Sandwich
Shakes and soups	Spinach Soup
Lunch	Grilled Lobster Tails
Salad	Pickled Sweet potato and Beetroot Salad
Dinner	Lemon Grilled Chicken
Dessert Smoothie	Peach Cobbler
	16th Day Plan
Breakfast	Fat Burning Smoothie + 1 Sandwich
Shakes and soups	Tomato Soup
Lunch	Avocado Sandwich
Salad	Tuna Salad
Dinner	Air Fryer Chicken Strips
Dessert Smoothie	Kiwi Splash
	17th Day Plan

Breakfast	Orange Detox Juice
Shakes and soups	Creamy Asparagus Soup
Lunch	Rosemary Grilled Salmon
Salad	Chicken Caesar Salad
Dinner	Crab Cake
Dessert Smoothie	Almond Shake
	18th Day Plan
Breakfast	Avocado Smoothie + 1 Sandwich
Shakes and soups	Vegetable Soup
Lunch	Dijon Baked Salmon
Salad	Papaya Kale Salad
Dinner	Rosemary Roasted Chicken
Dessert Smoothie	Coconut Cashew Protein Smoothie
	19th Day Plan
Breakfast	Strawberry Protein Smoothie + 1 Sandwich
Shakes and soups	Avocado Smoothie
Lunch	Potato Patty Sandwich
Salad	Shrimp Pasta Salad
Dinner	Chicken Stew
Dessert Smoothie	Chocolate Nut Smoothie
	20th Day Plan
Breakfast	Citrus Smoothie + 1 Sandwich
Shakes and soups	Pumpkin Soup
Lunch	Lemon Cod with Stir Fry Vegetables
Salad	Papaya Kale Salad
Dinner	Chicken Fajita
Dessert Smoothie	Almond Shake
	21st Day Plan
Breakfast	Fat Burning Watermelon Smoothie + 1 Sandwich
Shakes and soups	Butternut Squash Soup
Lunch	Smoked Trout
Salad	Julienne Cut Salad
Dinner	Deviled Eggs
Dessert Smoothie	Peach Cobbler
	22nd Day Plan
Breakfast	Blueberry Smoothie Bowl
Shakes and soups	Ginger Carrot Soup
Lunch	Buttery Garlic Shrimps
Salad	Red Cabbage and Carrot Salad
Dinner	243 Buttery Scallops

Dessert Smoothie	Avocado Shake
	23rd Day Plan
Breakfast	Cinnamon Apple Smoothie + 1 Sandwich
Shakes and soups	Strawberry Protein Smoothie
Lunch	Grilled Turkey Breast with Vegetables
Salad	Pickled Sweet potato and Beetroot Salad
Dinner	Zucchini Muffins
Dessert Smoothie	Banana Split
	24th Day Plan
Breakfast	Matcha Smoothie + 1 Sandwich
Shakes and soups	Lemon Lentil Soup
Lunch	Grilled Tuna Steak
Salad	Ultimate Fruit Salad
Dinner	Rosemary Roasted Chicken
Dessert Smoothie	Almond Shake
	25th Day Plan
Breakfast	Peanut Butter Smoothie
Shakes and soups	Detox Orange Smoothie
Lunch	Rosemary Grilled Salmon
Salad	Mexican Chicken Salad
Dinner	Stir-Fry Chicken
Dessert Smoothie	Kiwi Splash
	26th Day Plan
Breakfast	Raspberry Chia Smoothie Bowl
Shakes and soups	Butternut Squash Soup
Lunch	Grilled Chicken Sandwich
Salad	Chicken Fajita Salad
Dinner	Buttery Scallops
Dessert Smoothie	Banana Split
	27th Day Plan
Breakfast	Strawberry Smoothie + 1 Sandwich
Shakes and soups	Broccoli Soup
Lunch	Dijon Baked Salmon
Salad	Chicken Caesar Salad
Dinner	Lemon Grilled Chicken
Dessert Smoothie	Chocolate Nut Smoothie
	28th Day Plan
Breakfast	Orange Detox Juice + 1 Sandwich
Shakes and soups	Creamy Asparagus Soup

Lunch	Rosemary Grilled Salmon
Salad	Citrus Beetroot Salad
Dinner	Air Fryer Chicken Strips
Dessert Smoothie	Coconut Cashew Protein Smoothie

Made in the USA
Las Vegas, NV
05 June 2022

49816248R00136